Don't worry   Be Grumpy

DON'T WORRY

Inspiring Stories for Making the Most of Each Moment

BE GRUMPY

AJAHN BRAHM

WISDOM PUBLICATIONS • BOSTON

Wisdom Publications
199 Elm Street
Somerville, MA 02144 USA
www.wisdompubs.org

Library of Congress Cataloging-in-Publication Data
Ajahn Brahm, 1951– author.
  Don't worry be grumpy : stories for making the most of each moment / Ajahn Brahm.
    pages cm
  ISBN 978-1-61429-167-1 (pbk. : alk. paper)—ISBN 1-61429-167-5 (pbk. : alk. paper)—
ISBN 978-1-61429-184-8
  1. Buddhism—Anecdotes. I. Title.
  BQ4060.A53 2014
  294.3'4432—dc23
                        2014007178

          ISBN 9781614291671   ebook ISBN 9781614291848

18 17 16 15 14
5   4   3   2   1

Cover design by Phil Pascuzzo.
Interior design by Gopa&Ted2, Inc. Set in Scala Pro 10.5/16.

Wisdom Publications' books are printed on acid-free paper and
meet the guidelines for permanence and durability of the Production
Guidelines for Book Longevity of the Council on Library Resources.

This book was produced with environmental mindfulness. We have elected to print
this title on 30% PCW recycled paper. As a result, we have saved the following
resources: 25 trees, 11 million BTUs of energy, 2,151 lbs. of greenhouse gases, 11,665
gallons of water, and 781 lbs. of solid waste. For more information, please visit our
website, www.wisdompubs.org. This paper is also FSC® certified.

Printed in the United States of America.

MIX
Paper from
responsible sources
FSC® C011935

Please visit www.fscus.org.

contents

preface

Bananas are profound.

They are so commonplace we think we know everything about them. In fact, we don't even know the correct way to peel a banana! Most people peel the banana from the stalk. However, monkeys, the experts on bananas, always hold the stalk and peel their bananas from the opposite end. Try it and see. You'll find it much less troublesome following the "monkey method."

In the same way, meditating Buddhist monks and nuns are experts on separating the mind from the difficulties that surround it. I invite you to follow the "monk method" of dealing with life's problems. Like with peeling a banana, you'll find life much less troublesome.

1. The Container and the Contents

There were riots in the streets some years ago after a guard at Guantanamo Bay was accused of taking a holy book and flushing it down the toilet.

The next day, I took a call from a local journalist who told me he was writing an article about the outrage by asking leaders of all the major religions in Australia the same question he was about to ask me.

"What would you do, Ajahn Brahm, if someone took a Buddhist holy book and flushed it down *your* toilet?"

Without hesitation I answered, "Sir, if someone took a Buddhist holy book and flushed it down my toilet, the first thing I would do is call a plumber!"

When the journalist finished laughing, he confided that that was the first sensible answer he had received.

Then I went further.

I explained that someone may blow up many statues of the Buddha, burn down Buddhist temples, or kill Buddhist monks and nuns; they may destroy all this, but I will never allow them to destroy Buddhism. You may flush a holy book down the toilet, but I will never let you flush forgiveness, peace, and compassion down the toilet.

The book is not the religion. Nor is the statue, the building, or the priest. These are only the "containers."

What does the book teach us? What does the statue represent?

What qualities are the priests supposed to embody? These are the "contents."

When we recognize the difference between the container and the contents, then we will preserve the contents even when the container is being destroyed.

We can print more books, build more temples and statues, and even train more monks and nuns, but when we lose our love and respect for others and ourselves and replace it with violence, then the whole religion has gone down the toilet.

2. what we really want

The abbot woke up early one morning. Nothing unusual in that. But this morning he was awakened by the sound of something moving in the nearby shrine room. That *was* unusual because most of his monks would normally be practicing their morning "chanting" at this time ("Zzzzzz . . .") so he went to investigate.

In the darkness he saw a silhouette of a hooded figure. It was a burglar.

"What do you want, my friend?" said the abbot kindly.

"Gimme the key to the donation box, punk!" said the burglar brandishing a long, sharp knife.

The abbot saw the weapon but felt no fear. He felt only compassion for the young man.

"Certainly," he said, slowly handing over the key.

As the thief frantically emptied the box of cash, the abbot noticed the robber's jacket was torn, his face pale and gaunt.

"When was the last time you have eaten, dear boy?"

"Shuddup!" barked the burglar.

"You'll find some food in the cupboard next to the donation box. Help yourself."

The thief paused a moment in confusion. He was taken aback by the abbot's consideration for his welfare. Still, pointing the knife at the monk just in case, he hurriedly filled his pockets with cash from the donation box and food from the cupboard.

"And don't call the cops, or else!" he shouted.

"Why should I call the police?" answered the abbot calmly. "Those donations are to help poor people like you, and I have freely given you the food. You have stolen nothing. Go in peace."

The next day, the abbot explained what had happened to his fellow monks and to his lay committee. They were all very proud of their abbot.

A few days' later, the abbot read in the newspaper that the burglar had been caught robbing another house. This time he was sentenced to ten years in jail.

Just over ten years later, the same abbot was woken up early in the morning by the sound of someone in the shrine room. He got up to investigate and, yes you've guessed it, he saw the old burglar standing next to the donation box carrying a sharp knife.

"Remember me?" shouted the burglar.

"Yes," groaned the abbot reaching into his pocket. "Here's the key."

Then the burglar smiled, put down the knife, and said gently, "Sir, put away the key. I couldn't stop thinking about you all those long days in prison. You were the only person in my entire life who was kind to me, who actually cared about me. Yes, I have come back to steal again, but I realized that last time I took the wrong thing. This time I have come to take your secret of kindness and inner peace. That is what I really wanted in the first place. Please hand over the key to compassion. Make me your disciple."

Soon after, the thief became a monk and became rich beyond his wildest dreams. Not with money, but with a wealth of kindness and inner peace. That is what we all really want. What a steal!

3. Oh shit!

During a teaching trip to North America, I taught the following inspirational metaphor:

> When you step into some dog shit, don't get annoyed and wipe it off your shoes. Smile instead and take it back home. There you can scrape off the dog poo under the apple tree in your garden. Next year, those apples will be more plentiful, juicy, and sweet than ever before. But you must remember that when you bite into that succulent apple, what you are really eating is the dog shit! Only now it has been transformed into juicy, sweet apple.
>
> Similarly, when you experience any of the crises of life, it is like stepping into the dog shit. But instead of getting angry, bitter, or depressed, take it home with you and dig it into your heart. Soon you will be wiser and more compassionate. But remember, what is all that juicy wisdom and sweet love? It is just the dog shit of life transformed.

A couple of hours after delivering that awesome piece of advice, at a rest stop on the highway, I happened to step into some real dog shit. My driver, who had just heard the brilliant metaphor, refused to let me back into his vehicle until I had scraped every bit of the dog feces off both of my sandals. He literally pooh-poohed my dog-shit simile. That is the problem with many people these days. They live in apartments cut off from nature, with no garden to transform the shit into fruit.

4. Poo-sitive Reinforcement

Later during my visit to North America, someone told me where that dog poo had probably come from. A sharp businessman was making a fortune potty training pet dogs whose owners lived in city apartments.

Anyone who has had a new puppy in their house knows how troublesome it is to stop them doing their business on your expensive carpet. This businessman guaranteed to train every dog within three days to poo only outside. He used positive reinforcement.

He or his employee would take the pooch onto the street, to a tree or a small garden, and wait until the dog pood or peed. Then he would jump up and down shouting with glee, punching the air, dancing a jig, and singing a happy song. Sometimes the trainer would even do cartwheels. He would go way over the top in exuberant celebrations and extremes of ecstasy over the dog's excretions. It worked! That dog sensed that it had made someone very, very happy. Within three days, the dog would only poo outside. Such is the power of positive reinforcement, even on animals.

However, the dog trainer later got into big trouble. Some of his clients would be watching a game on TV, sitting quietly on the sofa with their dog. Then their team would score a spectacular touchdown or goal, and they would jump up off the sofa in glee, punch the air, dance a jig, and sing a happy song! And guess what the dog did?

5. The politician in the well

Sometimes in life, you don't step in the shit, someone throws it on top of you! The following story gives advice on what to do in such a situation.

A well-known politician with a dodgy reputation was strolling through the woods when he fell into a neglected well. Fortunately the well was dry, and his skull was so thick that he incurred no injury. Unfortunately, the well was too deep for him to climb out, so he screamed for help. Usually, a person becomes hoarse after yelling for a couple of hours, but being a professional politician with many years of experience, after three hours he was just getting into his stride.

Then a farmer came along, heard the noise, and discovered the politician at the bottom of the well.

"Help me!" said the politician.

"No way!" replied the farmer, recognizing him.

The farmer hated politicians, especially ultra-sleazy ones like this one. Moreover, he had always meant to fill that dangerous well. So he got out a spade and started shoveling dirt into the well. He would bury the politician and plug the well at the same time!

When the politician felt the mud being thrown on top of him, it was nothing unusual to him. Nevertheless, when he realized that the farmer's intention was to bury him alive, his screaming went to a higher level normally only heard at election time.

"I promise I will lower your taxes! I guarantee I will increase farm subsidies! I swear I will grant all cows free healthcare! Trust me!"

On hearing those words "Trust me!" the farmer began shoveling the dirt into the well even more vigorously. The politician began to shout more desperately. Then he went quiet.

The farmer thought that he had buried that politician and so carried on shoveling at an easier speed. The farmer was too busy shoveling to notice a strand of hair appear above the top of the well. As he shoveled more, the crown of a head could be seen. Then after he had put a little more earth in the well, he saw the smiling head of the politician. The farmer was now too shocked to carry on shoveling.

The politician had decided to stop complaining about having dirt thrown on him. Instead he'd shrug off the mud and compact it under his feet. After every shovelful of dirt, he would stand a few centimeters higher. Now he was high enough to climb out of the well and reward the farmer later with visits from the health inspectors and the tax collectors.

The moral of this story is that when life shovels shit on you, shrug it off, tread it in, and you will always stand higher in life.

6. Camel Face

Other people will sometimes get angry with you. Even your loved ones. It happens to all of us. Some people even got angry with the Buddha! So what can you do when you are on the receiving end of someone else's rage? The answer is to be found in the following story.

A husband was enjoying an afternoon off work at home. His wife was busy preparing dinner when she realized she was short of eggs.

"Darling," she asked, "would you mind going to the market and buying some eggs for me?"

"Sure, sweetheart," he happily replied.

The husband had never been to the market before. So his wife gave him some money, a basket, and the directions to the egg stall in the middle of the market.

When he entered the market, a young man came right up to him and shouted loudly, "Hello, Camel Face!"

"What!" replied the startled husband, "Who are you calling Camel Face?!"

But that only encouraged the young man, who started abusing the husband even more aggressively, "Hey Bat Breath! Did you use dog poo for aftershave this morning? May the fleas of a thousand stray dogs infest your armpits!"

Worst of all, the husband was being yelled at in public, in the middle of the market, and he had done nothing wrong at all. He got so upset and embarrassed that he turned around and walked out of the market as fast as he could.

"You're home early darling," remarked his wife on his return. "Did you get the eggs?"

"No!" huffed her husband. "And don't send me to that uncivilized, obnoxious, ill-mannered, toilet hole of a market ever again!"

Now the secret of a lasting marriage is to know how to smooth the ruffled feathers of your partner when he or she has just had a nasty experience. So his wife comforted and caressed him until the thermometer inside his heart registered a safer temperature. Then she softly asked him what that young man looked like.

Her husband screwed up his face and, between bouts of spitting indignation, gave a description of the young man.

"Oh, him!" said his wife, concealing a chuckle. "He does the same to everyone. You see, when he was a child, he fell over and hit his head. He suffered permanent brain damage, and he's been crazy like this ever since. Poor fellow, he couldn't go to school, he couldn't make any friends, he can't find a job, nor will he ever marry a nice girl and have a family. The unfortunate young man is mad. He shouts abuse at anyone and everyone. Don't take it personally."

After her husband heard that, his own indignation completely melted away. Now he felt compassion for the youth.

His wife noticed the change of heart and said, "Darling, I still need those eggs. Would you mind . . . ?"

"Sure, sweetheart," said the husband and he returned to the marketplace.

The young man saw him coming and shouted out, "Hey! Look who's coming! Old Camel Face has returned with his bat breath! Hold your noses everyone—a pile of dog shit on legs has just oozed into our marketplace!"

This time, the husband was not annoyed. He walked straight to the egg stall with the young man following him, hurling many an insult.

"Don't mind him," said the lady selling the eggs. "He does this to everyone. He's crazy. He had an accident when he was young."

"Yes, I know. Poor boy," said the husband as he paid for the eggs.

The young man followed the husband to the edge of the market, shouting ever-louder obscenities at him. But this time it never made the husband upset. Because he now knew that the young man was mad.

When you understand this story, then the next time that someone calls you terrible names, or your partner gets angry at you, just assume that they have hit their head today and are suffering momentary brain damage. For in Buddhism, getting angry at others and insulting them is called "temporary insanity."

When you realize that the person getting angry at you is temporarily insane, you are able to respond with equanimity and even compassion: "You poor thing!"

7. The Cracked Mug

The death of a loved one changes our lives forever. Even the deaths of those we don't know, such as the thousands who die in natural disasters, alters the way we think. Death is a fact of life, and when understood, it teaches us how to care.

Many years ago in Thailand, my teacher, Ajahn Chah, raised his ceramic mug.

"See this!" he told us. "It has a crack in it."

I looked closely at the mug but could see no crack.

"The crack is invisible now," Ajahn Chah continued, "but it's there. One day someone will drop this mug, and the crack will appear and split my mug apart. That is its destiny.

"But if my mug were made out of plastic," explained my teacher, "then it would have no such destiny and no invisible crack. You could drop it, knock it, or even kick it, and it would not break. You could be heedless because it was unbreakable. But because my mug is fragile, for that reason you must care for it.

"In the same way," Ajahn Chah began to emphasize, "your body has a crack in it. The crack is invisible right now, but it is there. It is called your future death. One day there will be an accident, a disease, or old age; then the crack will appear and you will die. That is your destiny.

"If your life lasted forever," Ajahn Chah concluded, "if your life were unbreakable like a plastic mug, then you could be heedless. So it is precisely because our lives are fragile, because it is our destiny to die, that we must care."

Understanding that relationships are also fragile like a ceramic mug is why we must care for each other. Comprehending that happiness has a crack in it teaches us to never to take joy for granted. Realizing that our lives will one day break apart makes us see that each moment is precious.

8. A Tale of Two Chicken Farmers

Once, there were two chicken farmers. The first rose early in the morning, picked up a basket, and went into the henhouse to collect the produce from the night before. He proceeded to fill his basket with chicken shit, leaving the eggs on the ground to rot. He then brought the basket of chicken shit back into the house, where it made a very bad smell. His family was very upset with that stupid chicken farmer.

The second chicken farmer picked up a basket and entered his henhouse also to collect the produce of the night before. But he filled his basket with eggs, leaving the chicken shit to rot in the shed. It would become valuable fertilizer later, but you don't bring it into the house with you! Bringing only the eggs back home, he cooked a delicious omelette for his family and later sold the remaining eggs in the market for cash. His family was very pleased with that clever chicken farmer.

The meaning of this parable is this. When you collect the produce of your past, what do you put in your basket and bring home with you? Are you one of those people who collect all the unpleasant experiences of today (or of your life) and bring them home with you: "Darling, I got pulled over for speeding today!" "Honey, the boss was really angry at me at work!" Or are you someone who leaves all those negative experiences in the past, where they belong, and only recollects the happy moments?

Are you a shit collector or an egg collector?

9. Your Photo Album

Many people have a photo album. In it they keep memories of the happiest of times. There may be a photo of them playing by the beach when they were very young. There may be the picture with their proud parents at their graduation ceremony. There will be many shots of their wedding that captures their love at one of its highest points. And there will be holiday snapshots too.

But you will never find in your album any photographs of miserable moments of your life. Absent is the photo of you outside the principal's office at school. Missing is any photo of you studying hard late into the night for your exams. No one that I know has a picture of their divorce in their album, nor one of them in a hospital bed terribly sick, nor stuck in busy traffic on the way to work on a Monday morning! Such depressing shots never find their way into anyone's photo album.

Yet there is another photo album that we keep in our heads called our memory. In that album, we include so many negative photographs. There you find so many snapshots of insulting arguments, many pictures of the times when you were so badly let down, and several montages of the occasions where you were treated cruelly. There are surprisingly few photos in that album of happy moments.

This is crazy!

So let's do a purge of the photo album in our head. Delete the uninspiring memories. Trash them. They do not belong in this album. In their place, put the same sort of memories that you have in a real photo album. Paste in the happiness of when you made up with your partner, when there was that unexpected moment of real kindness, or whenever the clouds parted and the sun shone with extraordinary beauty. Keep those photos in your memory. Then when you have a few spare moments, you will find yourself turning its pages with a smile, or even with laughter.

10. Pressing "Delete"

How do you delete the bad memories of the past?

Returning from the morning almsround in Thailand many years ago, Ajahn Chah picked up a stick by the side of the path and asked, "How heavy is this stick?" Before anyone answered, Ajahn Chah threw the stick into the bushes and said, "A stick is only heavy when you hold it. When you throw it away, the heaviness is gone."

Adapting this principle, I suggested to my own students that we perform the "stick ceremony." You write down on a piece of paper as many troublesome bad memories as you can recall. Then find a stick and wrap the piece of paper around one end of the stick, securing it with a rubber band or some tape. Next find a secluded place in the forest, hold the stick in your hand, and contemplate the weight of all those bad memories. When you are ready, with all the force that you can muster, throw that stick as far away as you can!

To let go of bad memories, you first have to acknowledge them. They need to be honestly recollected. Hence, writing them down on paper. Next, some physical act or ceremony is required to give the letting go some force. Simply thinking "I will now let this all go" does not work. The steps of wrapping the paper around the stick, walking into the forest with the purpose of letting the bad stuff go, feeling the weight of the stick in your grasp, and then the moment of release when you chuck it all away as far as you can: all these steps reinforce the intention. They give it power. It works. You have pressed the delete button.

Then someone complained that I was responsible for others making a mess in the forest. That I was encouraging environmental vandalism! So I adapted the strategy as follows:

Write out all the bad memories on a piece of paper as before. They need to be brought to the surface before they can be deleted. Only this time use a special type of paper, the most appropriate material for shitty memories. Write them out on a roll of toilet paper. When you have finished with the writing, take it to your bathroom, place the paper with the stinky writing in the toilet bowl where it belongs, and then flush!

11. Good? Bad? Who Knows?

A long time ago a king was out hunting when he cut his finger. He summoned his doctor, who always accompanied him on the hunt, and the doctor put a bandage over the wound.

"Is it going to be all right?" asked the king.

"Good? Bad? Who knows?" replied the doctor, and they carried on hunting.

By the time they had returned to the palace, the wound had become infected, and so the king summoned his doctor again. The doctor cleaned the wound, carefully applied some ointment, and then bandaged it.

"Are you sure it's going to be okay?" asked the king, becoming concerned.

"Good? Bad? Who knows?" replied the doctor again. The king became worried.

The king's worry was confirmed when, in a few days, the finger was so badly infected that the doctor had to amputate it! The king was so furious with his incompetent doctor that he personally escorted him to the dungeon and threw him in a cell.

"Well, Doctor, how do you like it, being in jail?"

"Being in prison, Sire . . . Good? Bad? Who knows?" replied the doctor with a shrug of his shoulders.

"You are insane as well as incompetent!" declared the king and departed.

A few weeks later, when the wound had healed, the king was out hunting again. Chasing an animal, he became separated from the others and ended up lost in the forest. Wandering in the woods, he was captured by the indigenous forest people. It was their holy day, and they had found a sacrifice for their jungle god! They tied the king to a large tree, and their priest began chanting and dancing as the forest people sharpened the sacrificial knife. The priest took the blade and was about to cut the king's throat when he shouted, "Stop! This man has only nine fingers. He is not perfect enough to sacrifice to our god. Set him free."

In a few days, the king found his way back to his palace and went straight to the dungeon to say thank you to the wise doctor.

"I thought you were stupid saying all this 'Good? Bad? Who knows?' nonsense. Now I know you were right. Losing my finger was good. It saved my life. But it was bad of me to lock you in jail. I'm sorry."

"What do you mean, Sire? Had you not put me in jail, I would have been there with you on the hunt, and I would have been captured too. And I have all my fingers!"

12. The Lost Taxi Driver

A man told me that in 1977 he was returning from a business trip to the Indian city of Mumbai. The trip had gone well, and he had ordered a taxi to take him to the international airport in plenty of time to check in. However, the taxi got lost. The driver, even though he was a local, couldn't find the way. As the minutes ticked by, the businessman was getting more and more concerned that he would miss his flight. He started getting angry at the taxi driver. The driver only got more confused.

Soon, the businessman realized that his only hope of catching his flight would be if it were delayed, which was quite common in those days. But when they finally approached the airport, his last hope was dashed. He saw his plane taking off. For once, the flight departed on schedule.

"You stupid taxi driver! You of all people should know the way to the airport. You should never again be allowed to drive taxis. You have made me miss my flight! You idiot!" shouted the businessman in a rage.

Then he looked up and watched as the aircraft fell from the sky. It crashed, and all on board were killed.

"You wonderful taxi driver! You are so wise. If only all taxi drivers were as clever as you. Please take a large tip!"

That man told me that the experience had changed his whole life.

He doesn't get so angry anymore when things do not go according to plan. Instead, he notes, "Good? Bad? Who knows?"

13. There Are No Criminals

I received a phone call from an officer at a local prison. He wanted to speak to me personally to invite me to come back to his prison to teach. I replied that I was very busy now with many more duties than in the old days when I used to visit regularly. I promised that I would send another monk.

"No!" he replied. "We want you."

"Why me?"

"I have worked in prisons most of my life," explained the guard, "and I have noticed something very unique with you. All of the prisoners who attended your classes never returned to jail once they were released. Please come back."

That is one of the compliments I treasure most. I thought about it afterward. What had I done that others hadn't that had genuinely reformed those in jail? I figured out that it was because, in all my years teaching in prisons, I had never once seen a criminal.

I have seen many people who had committed murder, but I have never seen a murderer. I have seen many people who had stolen from others, but I have never seen a thief. I have even seen people who had committed terrible sex crimes, but I have never seen a sex offender. I saw that the person was more than the crime.

It is irrational to define people by one or two, or even several, horrific acts that they have done. It denies the existence of all the other deeds that they have performed, the many noble acts. I recognized those other deeds. I saw peoplewho had done a crime, not criminals.

When I saw the people not the crimes, they also saw the good part of themselves. They began to have self-respect, without denying the crime. Their self-respect grew. When they left jail, they left for good.

14. The stigma of Mental Illness

I told the above story at a conference on mental health a few years ago. One of the department heads at a prestigious mental health facility was very impressed. He invited me to "bless" his building.

"What form of mental illness are you involved in?" I asked.

"Schizophrenia," he replied.

"And how do you treat the schizophrenia?" I enquired.

"Just like you explained in your presentation," he responded. "I don't treat the schizophrenia. I treat the other parts of the patients."

I raised my hands up in the Buddhist gesture of respect to him. He had understood.

"What are the results?" I asked, even though I knew what the answer would be.

"Brilliant! Much better than any other treatment," he answered.

When you call people schizophrenic, they are likely to live up to your label. You have stigmatized them. When you regard them as people who suffer episodes of schizophrenia, that they are more than their illness, then you give the healthy part a chance to grow.

15. Permission to Die

"Are you at peace with your impending death?"

I often say these words to people who are close to death. My aim is to convince them that it is okay to die, that there is nothing wrong with it. Then they can die with dignity and at peace.

Many such people tell me that they have already made peace with their coming death. The problem, they say, is that their relatives and close friends will not let them go. "Mother, mother, please don't die! Please get better. Please!" This becomes their greatest source of suffering.

Steve was a young Buddhist in his thirties. He had a successful tour company that took his clients whitewater rafting in some of the most beautiful locations in the world. Unfortunately, he was dying of an incurable cancer.

I had visited Steve and his wife, Jenny, many times and, honestly, was surprised that he hadn't passed away yet. He was suffering. Why was he hanging on?

I turned away from Steve, faced Jenny, and asked her, "Have you given Steve permission to die?"

What followed was one of those tingling moments in life that you feel forever privileged to have watched. Without giving me a reply, Jenny crawled up upon the bed, put her arms tenderly around her frail and emaciated husband, and told the man she loved to bits,

"Steve, I give you permission to die. It's all right Steve. You can go."
They hugged and cried. Less than two days later, Steve was dead.

Often I have to take aside the friends and relations of someone close
to death and suggest that they give to the one they love so much one
of love's greatest gifts: *permission to die*. That gift of freedom may only
be given in your own time and in your own way. It is the gift that
finally sets your loved ones free.

16. A Buddhist Joke

A Buddhist monk received a call from a lay member of his temple.

"Would you please come to my house today to perform a blessing?" the caller asked.

"I'm sorry," replied the monk, "I can't come because I'm busy."

"What are you doing?" inquired the caller.

"Nothing," replied the monk. "That is what monks are supposed to be doing."

"Okay," said the caller and hung up.

The lay Buddhist called again the following day. "Would you please come to my house today to perform a blessing?"

"I'm sorry," replied the monk, "I can't come because I'm busy."

"What are you doing?" asked the caller.

"Nothing," replied the monk.

"But that was what you were doing yesterday!" the caller complained.

"Yes," replied the monk, "but I'm not finished yet."

17. Old Monks Don't Lie

Every year, Buddhist monks of my tradition stop traveling and stay in one place for the three-month "rains retreat."

An old wandering monk arrived at the door of a poor farmer's cottage a few days before the start of the rains retreat. The husband, though poor, was a devout Buddhist and, having offered the monk some food, asked the monk to stay nearby for the retreat.

"I can build a simple hut for you, Venerable Sir, in a quiet meadow next to the river, and my wife will be happy to provide you with food. All that we ask is for you to teach us and guide us in meditation from time to time."

The old monk agreed.

Over the next three months, the farmer, his wife, and even their children got to love that wise and kindly old monk. So much so that at the end of the rains retreat, when the old monk told them he was leaving, the whole family cried and begged the old monk to stay.

"I cannot stay any longer," said the old monk. "However, because you have looked after me so well, I want to help you in return. A few days ago, in a very deep meditation, I saw that there is a huge treasure buried nearby. I want you to have it. Please listen carefully, follow my instructions, and you will never be poor again."

The whole family stopped crying. They listened intently. They believed that monk, because old monks don't lie.

"Stand at the threshold of your little cottage at dawn. Take up your bow and one arrow. Point the bow in the direction of the rising sun, and when the sun appears over the horizon, let the arrow fly. Where the arrow falls, there you will find the treasure."

The old monk left that evening. The following morning, the whole family was so excited that they were up well before dawn. The farmer stood at the threshold of his cottage with his bow and one arrow. His wife was carrying the spade. The sun, it seemed that morning, took forever to rise above the horizon, but when it finally rose, the farmer shot the arrow in the direction of the sun, and they all ran after it. When they reached the place where it fell, he told his wife to dig a hole. Deeper and deeper, she dug.

What did she find? Nothing! Only trouble! The arrow had landed in a field belonging to a rich man, and he caught them red-handed.

"You can't dig a hole in other people's property!" shouted the rich man at the poor wife. "I'll sue you! I'll send you straight to jail!"

"It's his fault," pleaded the wife, pointing to her husband. "He told me to dig here."

"It's the old monk's fault," said the husband. "He promised that we would find a treasure here."

"Old monk?" queried the rich man. "Well, old monks don't lie. What did he say to you?"

"Stand at the threshold of your little cottage at dawn. Take up your bow and one arrow. Point the bow in the direction of the rising sun, and when the sun appears over the horizon, let the arrow fly. Where the arrow falls, there you will find the treasure."

Having been told the old monk's instructions, the rich man exclaimed, "Oh, I know where you've gone wrong! Look at yourself, farmer. You're so poorly fed that you're too weak to shoot an arrow properly. I'll make a deal with you. Tomorrow, I will shoot the arrow from your cottage and, when we find the treasure, we'll split it fifty-fifty."

The farmer had little choice but to agree. So the following morning the rich man was holding the bow and arrow at the threshold, waiting for the sun to rise, and the husband was holding the spade. (It was his karma to dig today because he had made his wife dig yesterday!) When the sun appeared over the horizon, the rich man shot the arrow. It went much farther. They all ran after the arrow and, where it landed, the husband dug a big hole.

What did he find? Nothing! Only more trouble! The arrow had landed in a plot of land belonging to a general, and he captured them.

"You can't destroy my land!" screamed the general. "I'll order my soldiers to cut off your heads!"

"It's his fault," pleaded the farmer, pointing to the rich man. "He told me to dig here."

"It's the old monk's fault," said the rich man. "He promised that we would find a treasure here."

"Old monk?" queried the general. "Well, old monks don't lie. What did he say to you?"

"Stand at the threshold of your little cottage at dawn. Take up your bow and one arrow. Point the bow in the direction of the rising sun, and when the sun appears over the horizon, let the arrow fly. Where the arrow falls, there you will find the treasure."

Having listened to the old monk's instructions, the general declared, "Oh, I know where you've all gone wrong! What does a civilian know about shooting an arrow? Only a trained soldier like me can use a bow. I'll make a deal with you. Tomorrow, I'll shoot the arrow from your cottage, and when we find the treasure, we'll split it evenly three ways."

So the following morning the general was holding the bow and arrow at the threshold, waiting for the sun to rise, and the rich man was holding the spade. It was his karma to dig today. When the sun appeared over the horizon, the general expertly shot the arrow.

It went a very long way. They all ran after the arrow, and where it landed, the rich man had to dig a big hole.

What did he find? Nothing! Only more trouble! The arrow had landed in the garden of the royal palace, and the king's guards arrested all of them. Soon they were brought bound in chains before the king.

"It is a capital offence to destroy the royal garden," said the king. "What is the meaning of this?"

"It's his fault, Sire," said the general, pointing to the rich man.

"It's his fault, Your Majesty," said the rich man, pointing to the farmer.

"It's that old monk's fault, Your Highness," pleaded the farmer. "He said that we would find a treasure."

"Old monk?" queried the king. "Well, old monks don't lie. What did he say to you?"

"Stand at the threshold of your little cottage at dawn. Take up your bow and one arrow. Point the bow in the direction of the rising sun, and when the sun appears over the horizon, let the arrow fly. Where the arrow falls, there you will find the treasure."

When the king heard the old monk's instructions, he couldn't figure out what had gone wrong. So he sent out his soldiers to find that old monk and bring him back to the palace to explain. The monk was soon found and brought before the king.

"Old monk," said the king with respect. "You've got all these people into big trouble with your buried-treasure story. Explain yourself."

"Your Majesty, it is not a story. Old monks don't lie," explained the old monk. "They didn't find the treasure because they didn't listen."

"What part of the instructions didn't they follow?" asked the king, intrigued.

"Your Highness, why don't you come to the poor farmer's cottage tomorrow? I will show you how they all failed to follow my instructions. I will guarantee that you'll find the treasure, but I would ask that it be divided equally four ways between Your Majesty, the general, the rich man, and the farmer."

The king assented.

So it was that the farmer and his family, the rich man, the general, the old monk, and the king, were at the farmer's cottage early the next day. The old monk repeated the instructions.

"Stand at the threshold of your little cottage at dawn. Take up your bow and one arrow. Point the bow in the direction of the rising sun and, when the sun appears over the horizon, let the arrow fly. Where the arrow falls, there you will find the treasure."

As the king was standing at the threshold of the little cottage at dawn, he turned to the old monk for confirmation.

"Correct, Your Majesty," said the old monk.

The king took up the bow and one arrow.

"Correct, Your Majesty."

The king pointed the bow in the direction of the rising sun.

"Correct again, Your Majesty."

When the sun appeared over the horizon, the king was about to shoot the arrow when the old monk shouted, "Stop! Incorrect, Your Majesty."

The king stopped and stared at the old monk in confusion.

"*Listen*, Your Majesty. 'Let the arrow fly.'"

The king paused, repeating the words in his mind. Then, he began to smile. He had understood.

The king let go of the arrow and it flew straight down, landing right between his two feet, right where he was standing.

A shallow hole was dug, and they found such a large treasure that one quarter of it was enough to satisfy a king, not to mention the general and the rich man. How much more did it satisfy the poor farmer and his family!

The old monk further explained that when you shoot the "arrow of craving," aiming to find happiness, you usually find nothing, only more trouble. But if you let go of the arrow of wanting, it falls right where you are standing, in the here and now. There you will find the treasure of contentment, more than enough to satisfy even a king.

I can confirm this, because I'm an old monk, and old monks don't lie!

18. The Most Important Finger

The five fingers were arguing over who was the most important.

"I am the most important," said the thumb, "because I am the strongest. Also, when people approve of something they use me. I am the 'OK' finger!"

"No way!" said the index finger. "I am the most important. I am the finger of wisdom because I am used to point out things. Moreover, when people want to say 'number 1,' they use me."

"Ridiculous!" sneered the middle finger. "I am the biggest finger and can therefore see farther. I am so powerful that when people lift me up, others get very upset. Moreover, the Buddha taught that the way to enlightenment is the middle way, and I am the middle finger."

"I'm sorry but you are wrong," said the fourth finger kindly. "I am the most important because I am the finger of love. When people fall in love and get engaged, they put the ring on me. When they commit to care for each other in marriage, again they place the ring on me. I am the finger of love, love is the most powerful force in the world, and therefore I am the most important finger."

"Excuse me," interrupted the small finger. "I know that I am not tall or strong and am often ignored, but I believe that I am the most important finger. Although people use me to do dirty jobs, like removing wax from their ears, when they pray to the Buddha, I am always closest to the Buddha! Raise your hands, pray, and you will see."

In any community, family, or temple, the humble members who do the cleaning are the most important because, like the little finger, they are closest to the Buddha.

19. Describing Anxiety

I received a phone call from a student at Adelaide University. She had an acute case of anxiety. It was so bad that she was bedridden and terrified to go outside. The university doctors and psychologists had been unable to help her. So her uncle, a regular supporter of my monastery, told her to give me a call.

She told me over the phone that she had been bedridden for many weeks. She was managing thanks to her boyfriend, who cooked, cleaned, and did all other errands for her. Boyfriends like that are hard to find! Then I asked her, "Where on your body do you feel the anxiety when it occurs?"

"What do you mean?" she answered confused.

"Every emotion," I explained, "has a corresponding physical feeling. So where do you feel the anxiety?"

"I don't know," she replied.

"Well, find out and give me a call back when you can tell me."

A few days later, she called to tell me that she noticed a feeling in her middle chest, just below her breast.

"Describe that feeling to me," I asked.

"I can't," she replied.

"Well, give me a call back when you can describe it to me."

Three or four days later, she called and gave a surprisingly detailed description of the feeling in her chest that occurred whenever she had an anxiety attack.

"Very good," I complimented. "Now whenever you notice that physical feeling begin, put your hand on your chest and massage that area with as much kindness as you can generate for as long as you can. If you can't manage that in your current state, then get your boyfriend to massage that area for you. That's what boyfriends are for! And give me another call in a few days' time."

When she called, I asked her what happened to the physical feeling when she massaged it caringly.

"The physical feeling disappeared," she answered.

"And what happened to the emotion of anxiety?" I continued.

There was a pause.

"That went too!"

She now had the means to transcend her anxiety attacks. Asking her to locate the physical counterpart to her anxiety and to describe it to me was just a means to get her to be mindful of that feeling. Once awareness of that feeling had been established, it was a simple matter to relieve that feeling with compassion and, with it, abate the emotion of anxiety. I had also put her in charge of this therapy, restoring her self-confidence.

Every emotion has a counterpart physical feeling, often one that we are not aware of. Dealing with an emotional problem on the mental level is just too confusing, so we deal with the physical counterpart. Once the physical part is gone, so is its emotional source.

Within a short time she was out of bed and back in school. She was clever, worked hard, and graduated with honors. She was so impressed with me that she nominated me for Australian of the Year! I didn't win but appreciated the gesture. I appreciated even more when, in December 2009, at her insistence, I performed the marriage blessing for her and her groom, the same boyfriend who had cared for her earlier.

20. Kissing Pain Better

My parents were poor but kind. I grew up in a government-subsidized apartment called a *council flat*. We were not afraid of burglars. In fact, we used to leave our front door unlocked, hoping a burglar might enter, take pity on us, and leave us something!

I spent a lot of my youth playing soccer in the street with my friends. When I came off the worst in a tackle, I would scrape my knees on the stone pavement or hard asphalt. Bleeding and in pain, I would run to my mother in tears. She would simply kneel down and press her lips on the wound to "kiss it better." The pain would always go away. Then after quickly putting on a bandage, I was back kicking that soccer ball almost immediately.

Many years later, I wonder how unhealthy it was to place a mouth full of germs on an open wound! But it never led to an infection. Moreover, it was an instant painkiller.

I learned the healing power of kindness from my mother through incidents such as this.

21. The Tsunami Crocodile

Many amazing stories of survival came out of the 2004 tsunami. One of them is how kindness saved a Sri Lankan man's life.

Every morning, the man would go to the edge of a lagoon connected to the ocean to feed the fish with a loaf of sliced bread. One morning, a big crocodile appeared. Sri Lankan crocodiles are very dangerous. They are known to eat people.

Unfrightened, the kind man threw a few slices of bread to the crocodile. The croc snapped them up and swam away.

From that day on, the crocodile would come every morning for his breakfast of sliced bread and afterward swim away peacefully.

The man was feeding the fish the morning the tsunami came. Being close to the edge of the water, he was swept up in the strong currents and carried out to sea. At first, he tried to hold on to a wooden chair, but the forces of the tsunami were so strong that they tore the chair from his grasp. Then he grabbed on to another piece of wood, and that too was pulled away from him. Close to drowning, he grabbed on to a log of wood that was floating close to him. He managed to hold on to that and grab some air.

Coming back to his senses, he began to notice something very odd. Whereas every other object was being dragged by the current out to sea, his log was moving in the opposite direction back to the shore. When he was close enough to dry land, the man jumped off the log and scrambled up the bank to safety. Only then did he notice that his "log" had a tail. It was the crocodile!

Cynics say that the crocodile only saved the man so he could get some more bread the next morning. But the wise know that the crocodile was only repaying many acts of kindness with his own act of compassion.

22. Honey, I Can't Find the Kids!

I was fortunate to grow up in a small apartment. It meant that my parents, brother, and I couldn't escape from one another. My parents would argue like all married couples, but when they made up, I was there to see it. I learned that arguments are part of life, and that any bad feeling can easily be let go of in that beautiful act of forgiveness called "making up."

I shared a small bedroom with my elder brother. We fought together, got into trouble together, and grew up together, learning to love one another to bits. If I had had my own room, I would never have learned this.

I read in a newspaper about a woman in England who had won many millions of pounds in the lottery. She then brought a beautiful mansion in the countryside. One year later, she sold that impressive home at a loss and purchased a small house instead.

She explained that when living in her huge mansion, she could never find her children or her husband! Her son was in one wing of the sprawling house, her daughter was in another part, and her husband was in yet another set of rooms. They hardly ever saw one another. She was becoming lonely. The size of the mansion was separating her from her loved ones.

Now back in the small house, she sees her husband and kids all the time. She has lost the space of the mansion but rediscovered her family.

Maybe part of the problem of our rich, modern world is that we live in houses that are far too big. Each child has his or her own room. It is just too easy to escape from each other in such big houses. We become very adept at living on our own terms, but we don't learn the social skills of living with one another.

23. How a Mousetrap Killed a Chicken, a Pig, and a Cow

Five mice, a chicken, a pig, and a cow were friends and lived on a farm a long way from anywhere. The mice, who lived inside the farmhouse, would always help their friends. When one of the mice heard that the farmer wanted fried chicken, they would tell the chicken to hide. When they heard the farmer's wife planning a dinner of pork sausages, they would tell the pig to lie on its side and pretend to be sick. And when they heard that the farmer wanted a roast beef dinner, they would tell the cow to go off into another field. The chicken, pig, and cow called their five friends MI5—Mouse Intelligence Five.

One afternoon, one of the mice saw, through a crack in the wall, the farmer unpack a parcel. He almost squeaked his last breath when he saw that the parcel contained a mousetrap. "Oh no! We're toast! We're doomed!" he told the other mice. "What can we do?"

They all decided to go and ask their friend Mrs. Chicken for help.

"Kuk! Kuk! Kuk!" said Mrs. Chicken. "How can a little mousetrap hurt me?" The mice were so surprised that Mrs. Chicken would not consider helping them, nor even comfort them, after all the help the mice had given her.

So they went to see their friend Mr. Pig.

"Oink!" said Mr. Pig. "I'm a bit busy right now. I will get back to you later. After all, how can a mousetrap affect me?"

Again the mice were disappointed. So they went to see their biggest and bravest friend, Mrs. Cow.

Mrs. Cow was too busy chewing grass to even say "Moo!" Then, after much imploring from the anxious mice, she said, "Okay. I will ruminate on it, even though it is not *my* problem."

The mice returned home in dismay. After all the assistance they had given their friends, they got little more than a "Kuk! Kuk! Kuk!" from Mrs. Chicken, an "Oink!" from Mr. Pig, and not even a "Moo!" from Mrs. Cow.

Later that night, while searching for a midnight snack, one of the mice stepped in that mousetrap. "WHACCK!" and the mouse went straight up to heaven (because he had been kind).

The other four mice heard the sound and went to help. There was nothing they could do for their dear, deceased brother. They wept and they cried and they sobbed.

The farmer's wife also heard the sound of the mousetrap being sprung and went to investigate. When she saw the dead mouse with four other mice weeping with grief and taking turns holding one another in their little arms, she let out a scream and fainted.

By the next morning, she was still in shock and remained in bed. The farmer considered what he could give his wife to make her better. The thought came to him—chicken soup! So he caught Mrs. Chicken, decapitated her, and boiled her in a pot with some salt and garlic.

When the farmer's wife's friends heard that she was sick, they came to visit, as people do. The farmer had to feed his guests, so he slaughtered Mr. Pig and made him into grilled pork chops for his visitors.

Unfortunately, the farmer's wife never recovered from the shock of seeing four mice in grief. She died. A lot of people came for the funeral, and the farmer made many roast beef sandwiches for the mourners. Guess where that beef came from?

That is how a little mousetrap killed a chicken, a pig, and a cow. So never think, "It is not my problem." If your friend asks for help, it is your problem too. That's what friends are for.

24. How to Receive Praise

In 2004, I was awarded the prestigious John Curtin Medal—named after Australia's war-time Prime Minister—for exhibiting the qualities of vision, leadership, and community service in Australia. The presentation was made before dignitaries in Perth's Curtin University.

When I was asked to give a short acceptance speech, I stated that it was a great honor and a surprise, because there were others in the Australian community who had done much more service than I had done. I also emphasized that I could not have achieved so much without the huge support of so many others.

The following year, I received an invitation to attend the award ceremony for the 2005 winner. Thinking that if others attended my ceremony, then I should attend theirs, I went.

That year, the medal was awarded to Doctor Joske, the then-head of haematology at one of Perth's main hospitals. In his work with cancer sufferers, he had noticed that they received the world's best treatment in surgery, chemotherapy, and radiation therapy but inadequate aftercare. So he used his considerable influence to obtain a few rooms in the busy hospital to establish an alternative and complementary therapy center. There, anyone receiving conventional treatments for cancer could also receive acupuncture, foot massage, reiki, and other such treatments generally considered unscientific, all free of charge. He reasoned that, at the very least, the patients would receive comfort and relief and feel cared for when, say, someone massaged their feet for thirty minutes. Ridiculed by his fellow doctors, he pressed ahead and had remarkable positive results. I was inspired by his story.

Then Doctor Joske was asked to give his acceptance speech. He said that it was a great honor and a surprise, because there were others in the Australian community who do much more than he had done. He also pointed out that he could not have achieved so much without the huge support of so many others.

Sitting in the audience, I thought, "Hey! That's my speech from last year." Indeed it was. It is most people's speech when given praise in public.

In Doctor Joske's case, I was absolutely convinced that he well deserved the recognition that the John Curtin Medal gives. It made me think, "Perhaps, conceivably, I also deserved the previous year's award? Many highly intelligent academics had thoroughly researched my work and its outcomes and decided I was worthy. What right had I to question their wise and informed judgment?" I concluded that yes, just as Doctor Joske deserved his award, so I deserved my medal. Only then did I receive the praise, albeit one year late.

Now when intelligent people give me praise, I pay due respect to their wisdom by receiving the praise, saying, "Thank you. I deserve that."

My response makes people laugh because it is unusual, but they get the point and begin to accept praise themselves. It makes such a huge difference to their emotional well-being.

As a postscript, I previously rejected praise because I had been taught that it would give me a big head. It does not. Instead, receiving praise gives you a big heart.

25. The Fifteen Seconds of Praise Rule

Experiments in psychology have shown that it takes on average fifteen seconds of continuous praise for it to be heard. But criticism is received immediately!

We are so uneasy with receiving praise that we usually reject it with thoughts such as:

"What is she on about?"

"Is he drunk or just plain crazy?"

"Okay, there's some hidden motive behind this."

Therefore, if you want to tell your wife what a wonderful woman she is, or tell your husband how much you admire him, then get out a stopwatch or look at the clock and *keep going*. Only after fifteen seconds will they take the praise seriously!!

26. The Sandwich Method

When we do need to criticize people, what often happens is that we do it so unskillfully that they get offended, we feel bad, and so we avoid giving any more feedback in future. The original problem gets worse.

Imagine a business where a manager is too reluctant to point out a fault in a worker because she doesn't like conflict. The business will suffer. Suppose the coach of a sports team delays criticizing one of the player's failings because he is afraid of creating discord. The team will lose. It is our duty to give timely criticism. Here is how it is done.

First, praise the people you want to criticize. Lay it on thick but honestly. The purpose of the praise is to establish that we respect them, value their contributions, and that we are not simply putting them down.

Praise also serves to open up people's ears. We pay scant attention to what people are saying to us, preferring to listen to our own thoughts about what they are saying instead. Praise is the bait that lures us out of our self-protective inner safety room so we can fully hear what is being said. We like praise, so our ears open wider for more.

Then we hit them, metaphorically of course, with the criticism, "But . . ." And the reprimand goes in through opened ears.

Lastly, we add another thick layer of praise, reinforcing that we are not rejecting them as people, only pointing out one or two faults among so many good qualities that we have just now taken the time to point out.

The result is that the offender accepts the criticism without feeling diminished, we as manager have performed our job with no unpleasant aftertaste, and the problem has been addressed.

The first wad of praise is the top slice of bread in the sandwich, and the last layer of praise is the bottom slice. The criticism is the filling. Thus it's called the "sandwich method."

27. The 70-Percent Rule

Before I became a monk, I was a teacher in a British high school. Teaching teenagers is enough stress to make anyone think of renouncing the world and becoming a monk!

When I had to give my first exam in mathematics, I asked a senior teacher for advice. He told me not to make it too hard, because if the average score is 30–40 percent, the students will become discouraged. They will start thinking that math is too difficult and give up. Conversely, if the test is too easy and the average mark is 90–100, then the test would be pointless.

So he advised me to set the test aiming for an average score of 70. That way the students will be encouraged in their ability to do well at mathematics and, in the 30 percent of the test where they make mistakes, I would be able to identify their weak points and address those in their next lessons. The exam was 70 percent for encouragement and 30 percent for learning.

Later, I realized that the same applies to life. If your average score in life's tests is only 30–40 percent, then you will become discouraged, even depressed, and give up. And if you always score 95–100 in life, you learn very little and stagnate. But if your life's score is around the magical 70 percent, then you have enough success to retain your motivation and enough failure to learn and grow as a person.

28. Lower Your Expectations

The 70-percent rule demonstrates why we should never expect 100 percent in life. It shows why it is all right for you to fail sometimes. Aim to fail 30 percent of the time, and you will have a rich life. Aim not to fail at all and you will be so stressed, afraid, and controlling that you won't have much of a life at all. So lower your expectations to 70 percent and start enjoying life.

We have such high expectations of our husbands and wives that we find it hard to enjoy a long-lasting relationship where we both feel accepted enough to grow. So if your husband only scores 70, *keep him*! If your wife scores 98, tell her to relax more and make some mistakes or you will dump her!

Parents should lower their expectations of their children. Only half of all children can come in the top 50 percent at school! And children should lower their expectations of their parents too. None of us has finished growing yet.

In fact, I often advise Buddhist parents that if their children come in the top 10 percent or bottom 10 percent at school or college, then they are not good Buddhists. This is because good Buddhists should follow the core teaching of the Middle Way. If your kid comes in the middle somewhere, then they are good Buddhists!

Boys want good-looking girlfriends. Girls want rich husbands. They should both lower their expectations for a happier life. When a boy marries a beautiful girl, he will be jealous for the rest of his life, worried that she may be seduced by another man. But if he marries an ugly girl, he has nothing to worry about. If a girl marries a rich guy, she will always be suspicious that he may be having an affair with another woman. But if she marries a poor guy, then he will never be able to afford a mistress, so her marriage is secure, and she can relax. This is another example where lowering expectations makes life easier and more fun.

29. Three of My Most Memorable Mistakes

I don't expect to be perfect. In fact, I like making mistakes. Because when I tell my friends about the stupid things that I have done, it makes them laugh. My stupidity increases the happiness in the world.

1. I had just completed teaching a nine-day meditation retreat in Penang, and my hosts were seeing me off at the airport. They had bought me a yummy coffee drink before I was to board the aircraft. It was strong, thick, and sweetened with ice cream.

I went to suck the delicious nectar through the straw, but nothing came through. I sucked harder. Still nothing. The straw must be blocked. So I sucked really hard. That was when I noticed some of my hosts giggling while the others were holding their hands over their mouths trying, out of politeness, not to laugh. So I removed the straw from the glass, only to realize that it was a plastic spoon.

Where I came from, spoons were metal with wide flat handles, not thin, round, and plastic as in modern coffee shops. And the coffee was too thick to see what was on the end of the plastic thing. Nevertheless, I burst out laughing, allowing my hosts to join in. I had made many people happy.

2. My early training as a Buddhist monk occurred in northeast Thai-

land under the renowned meditation teacher Ajahn Chah. When I arrived in Thailand, I could speak no Thai, so I had to learn "on the job."

One day I needed some soap. The routine was to approach the teacher and simply ask, in Thai of course. The Thai word for soap is *saboo*. I said "sapo," which happens to mean "pineapple."

Ajahn Chah asked what I wanted a pineapple for. I answered "to wash with." Ajahn Chah almost fell off his chair laughing.

He had merriment for days telling his Thai visitors, "Have you seen these Westerners? They wash with pineapples. They're such an advanced culture."

My attempts to speak Thai gave many such happy moments to my teacher.

3. On another occasion, I was asked to perform the funeral ceremony for the parent of a Sri Lankan member of my Buddhist temple. I stood at the lectern in the funeral home to welcome all the mourners to the solemn Buddhist ceremony. I began by saying, "We are here today to remember with respect my friend's mother, who passed away recently."

Sri Lankan names are so long and difficult for Westerners to pronounce that I called her "my friend's mother."

It was then that an old lady sitting in the front stood up, interrupted my welcoming speech, and said indignantly, "It is not me who has died; it's my husband!"

Everyone laughed. I think even the coffin shook! The service then became a true celebration of the life of the deceased, full of happy memories to the very last.

30. The Last Question

I received a call late in the afternoon that a Buddhist family was on its way to see me after finishing interviews with the police. That morning, they had woken up to a parent's worst nightmare. They found their seventeen-year-old son hanging on the end of a rope.

Often suicides among the young are totally unpredictable. The boy had many friends and showed no signs of depression. He appeared happy at school, where he was about to take the university entrance exams. He was expected to perform very well. There was not the slightest forewarning of what he was about to do.

The parents were struggling with guilt, asking themselves repeatedly what they could have done, or said, to prevent this. Fortunately, Buddhism doesn't exaggerate personal mistakes and nurture them into the devouring monster that is guilt. I could easily reassure them that they deserved no blame. Such suicides happen to the most caring and diligent of parents. They accepted this.

Next, they expressed a level of concern that I can only describe as "terrified" over what would happen to their son after such a death. Being Buddhists, they accepted reincarnation. They had also heard that those who commit suicide are reborn in hell.

It was trauma enough to witness the suicide of their son, but imagining him in such terrible pain afterward was adding torment upon torture. Whether or not we believe in life after death, we all like to hear that our recently deceased loved ones "have gone on to a happier place." Imagine what it must be like to believe that they are now in a far worse place, an indescribably worse place.

Knowing that their son would have been taking his university entrance exams soon, I asked the parents how many subjects he was to take and how many papers in each subject. The parents were confused about why I was asking such a question at this time. Out of respect for me, they replied that he was to take four subjects with two papers in each. Then I asked how many questions, on average, in each paper. They replied that there were about eight questions per paper.

"That makes a total of sixty-four questions to get into an Australian university," I said. "What would happen if a student answers sixty-three of those questions perfectly correct but makes a total mess of the very last question? Would that student get accepted into university?"

The parents smiled as they said, "Yes, of course." They had understood the metaphor.

Their son does not get denied a happy rebirth solely because of his suicide, no more than a student is denied a place at university solely because he gave a wrong answer to the last question on the exam. Their son was a very kind, good boy. He had given so many excellent answers to the tests of life that he well deserved a happy rebirth.

31. The Benefits of Being Blown Up

I travel in planes a lot—so frequently that many of my friends worry for my safety. Planes are a prime target for terrorists, and the more I step on a plane, the more likely a suicide bomber will blow me up.

In order to reassure my friends, I recount the three benefits of dying in an aircraft explosion at thirty thousand feet:

1. *Instant cremation.* If you have ever had to organize the funeral of a close relation, you will know how much work it is. You have to organize the funeral company, select the coffin, inform all the friends and relatives, take time off work for the ceremony, and, usually, feed your guests afterward. But if your grandma, for example, dies in a bomb explosion in mid flight, everything is taken care of. No need for funeral directors, coffins, or taking time off work. Even the scattering of the ashes is taken care of. This is the first benefit: an instant and worry-free cremation.

2. *Cost-effective outcome.* Funeral services, as they say, cost an arm and a leg (and the rest of the body for the one in the box). The relatives organizing the rites, understandably, cannot bring themselves to arrange a cut-price, special-offer-for-this-week-only funeral for dear old grandma. But if grandma died in an aircraft terrorist attack, not only would there be no funeral expenses, but the relations would get a substantial

insurance payout from the airline company as well. At the end of the day, they would come out ahead from granny's demise.

3. *Fortunate next life.* The best benefit is the last. If grandma expires in an aircraft explosion at thirty thousand feet, she passes away so close to heaven that it is fairly easy for her to go the rest of the way.

These are the reasons I'm not at all afraid of flying. It's another example of overcoming anxiety with positive thinking.

32. Should I? Shouldn't I?

At the end of my lecture in Oslo, a young woman I had never seen before asked me a question on how one should make important decisions in life.

In order to ground her question in reality, I replied, "Well, suppose someone were trying to decide whether to marry her boyfriend?"

The poor girl blushed bright red, held her head in her hands, and turned in extreme embarrassment to her boyfriend sitting next to her! The audience didn't help by their bursting into laughter.

After apologizing, I introduced an old method for making decisions with an unexpected new meaning: Toss a coin! Heads I marry him. Tails I don't.

The new meaning, which I had only heard of recently, comes from paying close attention to your emotional reaction at the result.

Suppose it comes up heads, meaning, "I marry him." Do you react with a "Yeah!" and grin happily or with "Hmm! Maybe I'll try two out of three" and frown with disappointment? The reaction tells you very clearly what you really want to do. Whatever that is, you follow it.

Tossing a coin is simply a very effective way of finding out what your heart is telling you.

33. Ask Your Dog

We love our pets very much. So one of the hardest decisions a pet owner will one day have to make comes when the veterinarian asks for approval to euthanize a sick pet.

Consenting to killing a well-loved pet seems heartless, and for a Buddhist, it breaks a core moral precept. Yet preventing the vet from ending your pet's suffering appears even more cruel. How do we solve this moral dilemma?

Easy. Ask the dog!

Judy took her cancer-stricken dog to the vet yet again. The doctor said that there was nothing more he could do except to give the suffering dog the final needle. Judy asked for a few moments alone with her dear little dog. Many times she had heard me give the advice to "ask the dog." So she cradled her cherished companion in her arms, looked deep into her eyes, and asked, "Do you want to die now? Have you had enough of this cancer? Or would you like to continue on a little longer?"

When you have lived with a pet for a long time and formed a loving relationship, you will know what the pet wants. Judy felt very strongly that her trusting little dog did not want her life ended yet. So she told the vet "no."

The vet became angry. "You Buddhists are so cruel and stupid!" But there was nothing the vet could do. Judy took her dog home.

A few months later, Judy took the same little dog back to visit the vet. It had made a full recovery all on its own. Even cancers in humans vanish unexpectedly sometimes. The vet was amazed and, after checking the dog thoroughly to confirm it really was in good health, said, "You Buddhists are so compassionate and wise!"

It is not our duty to decide on the life or death of another, not even of an animal. Our role is to ask our pet. Any loving owner will know the answer once it has been asked. Then we convey that message to the vet. It is your dog's decision, or your cat's, not yours. They know.

34. Caring, Not Curing

I have been living in Perth as a monk since 1983. Over those years, I have gained the trust and respect of the local Buddhist families to the point where I am regarded as a sort of honorary grandpa to many young men and women. They have grown up coming to my temple and feel comfortable sharing secrets with me that they would never tell their parents!

Such a one was the distressed young doctor who came to see me. He had recently begun work as an intern in one of the big hospitals in Perth. The previous day he had lost his first patient in tragic circumstances. A young female patient of his had died. He had to tell her inconsolable husband that his young wife was dead and that his two small kids have no mum any more. The new doctor felt so guilty that he had failed that young family.

Of course, he was not to blame. He had done everything for his patient that was medically possible. The reason why he felt he had failed was due to something else, and that is what I spoke to him about.

"If you believe that your duty as a doctor is to cure your patient, then you are going to suffer this same failure again and again. During your career, many of your patients will die. But if you accept that your main duty is to care for your patients, then you never need to fail. Even though you may not be able to cure them, you will always be able to care for them."

As he was an intelligent young man, he understood immediately and soon became a much better doctor. His main goal became to care for his patients. If his patients were cured, that was a wonderful bonus, but if they died, then they passed away in the warmth of being cared for.

Many of the appalling medical interventions that health professionals inflict on their patients, desperately trying to keep them alive when death is inevitable, occur because our society values curing above caring. Not only would many people's last moments be more comfortable and peaceful if we emphasized caring more than curing, I think that more patients would be cured as well!

35. Milk and Cookies

A senior surgeon in a prestigious American hospital examined the referred woman's medical record. Her cancer was advanced, and every other hospital in the region had given up on her. Any treatment would be complex, expensive, and there was only a small chance that she would survive. Having checked her details, and after making a few more inquiries, he took on the difficult case.

His fellow doctors were surprised at the amount of resources he was willing to commit to the treatment of this woman. He called in many favors in order to assemble top specialists from other parts of the country and dedicated so much of his limited time and energy to helping this one patient.

The doctor's extraordinary efforts paid off. At the end of many months, he could tell her that the cancer was in full remission and that she could expect to live many more happy years. She was overjoyed.

A few days later, she received the bill from the hospital in the mail. She opened the envelope with dread, expecting to see a fee for many hundreds of thousands of dollars. Instead, she saw in her doctor's own handwriting:

Paid twenty-five years ago with a glass of milk and two cookies.

Twenty-five years previously, that doctor had been a poor medical student, trying to pay his way through college doing odd jobs. One such job was as a door-to-door salesman. Late one hot afternoon, having sold nothing all day, he knocked on yet another door and a woman opened it. She listened to his worn sales pitch and declined to buy anything. But then she asked the tired looking young man, "Have you had anything to eat yet?"

"Not since breakfast, ma'am."

"Then just you wait here," she said, and she quickly returned with a glass of milk and two cookies for the exhausted young med student.

Twenty-five years later, that student was a senior surgeon at a prestigious hospital. When he examined the woman's medical record, her name rang a bell. A few phone calls confirmed that she was indeed the kind lady who had given him the welcome snack.

Out of gratitude for a little act of kindness many years before, never forgotten, not only did he go the extra distance to make sure she survived the cancer, but he also paid her bill.

36. The Guilt of a salesman

When I was a student, and my hair was much, much longer than it is today, I also took odd jobs during the university holidays to make ends meet. One such job was selling children's encyclopedias door to door.

First I had to learn the marketing pitch. It was a short speech that I had to memorize, which argued persuasively that not to purchase this amazing source of knowledge would be to deny a proper education to your dear child. I was instructed to use psychological pressure to make the parents feel almost as guilty as child abusers if they irresponsibly chose not buy this magnificent set of educational books.

Such a hard sell was immoral. I knew it. But I was young and desperate.

The first day, I sold a set to this sweet young couple who had recently moved in to a new house with their two very young children. That night I did not sleep well at all. I kept thinking of those young parents saddled with another bill to pay because I sold them this stupid, rubbish encyclopedia. I felt so guilty that I resigned the next morning.

For many years I felt very remorseful over that sale. Later, as a monk, I learned to forgive myself and let it go. After all, I was so immature in my long-haired days.

I once mentioned this anecdote in a Friday night talk in Perth as an example of forgiveness. Afterward, a young woman in her late twenties came to talk with me.

"You may not believe me, but this is absolutely true!" she began. "When I was a very young girl growing up in London, a young long-haired student came to our house and sold my Mum and Dad this children's encyclopedia. I simply *loved* those books!" she enthused. "They were my favorite books of all. It may not have been you, but thank you so much anyway." For once I was speechless.

The way I now understand how this universe works, I am pretty sure that it was I who sold her parents those books.

37. The sad saga of the suicidal spider

A young, happy spider found the perfect corner in a quiet room in which to build her first home. Joyfully she spun and wove a beautiful web, artistic enough to be featured in *Spiderworld's Home and Garden*. Exhausted but proud of her efforts, the young spider rested in the center of her web, waiting for lunch.

An elderly woman entered the room, and on seeing the spider, she screamed so loud even her half-deaf husband heard it. On seeing the cause of her distress, the husband quickly smashed the spider's first home to smithereens. The spider was lucky to escape with her life.

Rattled but undaunted, the spider crawled to another house and built a second home, this time not as aesthetic as her first web, but comely enough. Before the spider's first meal arrived by air, a maid spotted the web and destroyed it with her broom. Again the poor spider fled for her life.

The same thing happened in the next house, and the next, and the next one after that. After her sixth web was violently destroyed, the poor little spider understandably began to suffer the symptoms of posttraumatic stress disorder. She became paranoid of corners, too anxious to spin any more webs.

As she crawled tired and hungry along the road, she became lost in negative thoughts: "No one likes me. All I want is a quiet home somewhere. I won't harm anyone; I just want to catch flies and bugs.

They don't want the bugs anyway. Life is so unfair. I'm hungry. I'm tired. I feel so . . . so alone."

Then the little spider began to cry.

Soon her thoughts turned to suicide. "Nobody loves me. What's the point of going on? I'll never find a home. I'll never get food. Maybe I'll kill myself."

The suicidal spider deliberately crawled under the shoes of the passing pedestrians, but she always managed to find herself in the safe space between the heel and the sole. Then she crawled across the busy road but always went between the wheels, never underneath them. When you're depressed, you can't do anything right, not even suicide.

Suicidal spider soon gave up even trying to kill herself. Sobbing and sniffling, she staggered along the road like a drunk, not aware of where she was going. Soon, she felt someone looking at her. She stopped and turned to see a big fat happy spider smiling kindly at her.

"Why are you crying?" asked the fat happy spider.

Wiping her nose with a tissue, she told the sad story of her life. After suicidal spider finished her tale of woe, she suddenly realized that not all spiders were thin and depressed. This one was fat and looked very happy.

"How come you're so fat and happy?" asked suicidal spider.

The fat spider smiled softly.

"Didn't anyone destroy your webs when you built them?"

"I only ever built one web in my whole long life," the spider replied. "I catch plenty of food every day. In fact," continued fat happy spider, compassionately, "there is more than enough for the two of us. Come and live with me."

"Wait a moment," said suicidal spider. "Where on earth have you built such a web that no one has disturbed it for such a long time?"

"Oh!" replied fat happy spider, "I built my web in the donation box at Ajahn Brahm's temple. Nothing ever disturbs me there!"

38. The Secret to a Happy Marriage

Why is it that many priests and monks perform marriage rites when they themselves are celibate? I have conducted many marriage ceremonies in my time. Once I even performed a celebrity wedding and had my photo appear in the Malaysian edition of the gossip magazine *Hello*!

During the ceremony, I have to give the dewy-eyed young couple some wise words of advice. I do this out of selfishness. I don't want the couple, who I have just married, to keep bothering me later with their marital problems. So at the ceremony I tell them "The Secret" to a happy marriage and then they leave me alone. I am happy. They are happy. It's a win-win!

So what is "The Secret" to a happy marriage?

At the right moment in the proceedings, usually after the rings have been exchanged, I look into the eyes of the new bride and tell her, "You are a married woman now. From this moment on, you must never think of yourself." She immediately nods and smiles sweetly.

Then I look at the groom and say, "You are now a married man. You also must not think of yourself anymore." I don't know what it is about guys, but the groom usually pauses for a few seconds before saying "Yes."

Still looking at the groom, I continue, "And from this time on, you must never think of your wife." Then quickly turning to the bride, I say to her, "And you must not think of your husband from now on."

I enjoy watching the confused expressions appear on the couple's faces. You don't have to be a mind reader to know what they are thinking: "What is this crazy monk on about!"

Confusion is a very effective teaching device. Once people are engaged in trying to solve a riddle, then you can teach them the answer and they pay attention.

"Once you are married," I explain, "you should not think of your-selves; otherwise you will be making no contribution to your marriage. Also, once you are married, you should not always think of your partner; otherwise you will be only be giving, giving, giving, until there's nothing left in your marriage.

"Instead, once you are married, think only of 'us.' You are in this together."

The couple then turn to each other and smile. They get it straight away. Marriage is about "us," not about me, not about him, not about her.

To make sure they understand "The Secret," I ask them, "When any problem arises in your marriage, whose problem is it?"

"Our problem," they answer together.

"Very good!" I say with a grin.

In a relationship, if a problem arises and you think that is your part-ner's problem, you will not be contributing to a solution. When you think that it is your own problem, then you will neglect half of the solution. But when every difficulty is regarded as "our" problem, you will find solutions together. That creates a rich and happy marriage.

39. Holy water

Another part of the Buddhist wedding ceremony is sprinkling the happy couple with holy water—for good luck. Actually marriages these days need all the luck that they can get, so I usually drench them in it! When much of the bride's makeup begins to dissolve, with mascara dribbling down her cheeks, I explain to the husband, "Now you can see what she really looks like!" Better he finds out now than later, I say.

Coming in from overseas to Perth Airport one day, I read the full version of the Australian customs regulations. I was surprised to read that one of the items that you are prohibited to import into Australia is holy water. Check it out! Perhaps this is the reason for such a prohibition:

In the good old days when Australian airports had a "green channel" through which you could just walk out of the airport, an Australian traveler was stopped at random. When the customs officers opened his suitcase, they found two bottles of undeclared whiskey hidden under the jackets and trousers.

"What are these?" asked an officer.

"I am a religious man," said the traveler thinking quickly. "I have just returned from a pilgrimage to the holy site of Lourdes in France. This is only holy water."

"Hmm," replied the customs officer, "then why does it say Johnny Walker on the label?"

"I had to carry the holy water in something. These were two empty bottles that I used, okay? Can I go now?"

The suspicious customs officer decided to open one of the bottles to test it. He held it up to his nose and declared, "This isn't holy water. It's whiskey! Smell it for yourself."

The traveler put the bottle to his nose, took a whiff, and exclaimed, "My God! You are right. It must be another miracle. Hallelujah!"

And from that time on, maybe, holy water became an item that people were prohibited from bringing in to Australia.

40. The Dangers of Driving Drunk

Buddhist monks are not allowed to turn water into wine, which may be why there are more Christians than Buddhists in Australia.

Many years ago, a man in Sydney decided to drive home after an office party where he had had too many beers. He reckoned there was a very good chance he wouldn't get caught.

That evening however, the Sydney police had established a roadblock on a popular route to check the alcohol level of every driver. As luck would have it, the roadblock was on this man's way home, and seeing the roadblock up ahead, he realized he was trapped. There was no way out.

He pulled over, waiting in line to be tested, and he resigned himself to being heavily fined, or maybe even losing his driver's license. All he could do was to wait for the inevitable misery and humiliation. He felt the darkness of doom about to swallow him, and he sat glumly, cursing his bad luck.

When it got to his turn for testing, the officer asked him to step out of his car and handed him a breathalyzer to blow into.

He took the machine and was about to blow into it, when just at that moment, there was a loud CRASH! A vehicle pulling over at the roadblock had slowed down suddenly at the roadblock and had been rear-ended by the car behind. The officer took back the device, saying, "I have to attend to this accident. Get back in your car and go home."

Stunned and in disbelief, he spun around, stumbled into the driver's seat, put his foot on the pedal, and made a swift exit, singing to himself all the way home.

The following morning, he awoke to the sound of his doorbell. As he crawled out of bed to dress, he held his throbbing head, for he had a terrible hangover from all the partying the night before. A few minutes later, after stumbling down the stairs, he opened his front door to see two large Sydney policemen standing outside.

He was alarmed at first, but then he thought, "They can't arrest me now. I'm not driving."

"Good morning, officers," he said, collecting himself. "What seems to be the problem?"

"Good morning, sir. Would you mind if we took a look inside your garage?"

He thought for a moment. He had nothing to hide. So what the hell?

"Of course," he replied with a smile. "I always like to be of assistance to our local police force. Come with me." And he strode confidently toward the garage.

But when he opened the garage door, his face went white, his lips began to quiver, and his eyes bulged so far they almost came out of their sockets. For inside his garage . . . there was a police car! He'd driven the wrong car home!

Such are the dangers of drunk driving.

41. Holy shit

People today assume that life has changed so much since ancient times. However, looking through some of the old stories of Buddhist monks and nuns misbehaving 2,500 years ago in India, it is clear that some things never change.

In a nuns' monastery in the time of the Buddha, long before the days of sewage pipes, it was one nun's job to empty out the buckets that collected the feces and other waste from the monastery toilets. Early one morning, instead of disposing of the waste in the designated spot, the negligent nun threw the excrement over the monastery wall.

As it happened, a well-dressed businessman on his way to the palace to meet the king was walking on the other side of the wall that morning. Whatever that man was thinking soon changed when a bucket of shit fell on his head.

He was upset. He was incensed. He was infuriated.

Knowing where the bucket of filth had come from, he shouted, "Those aren't real nuns! They're just old crones and hookers! I'll burn their monastery down!"

Taking up one of the flaming torches used to light the street in early morning, he strode into the nuns monastery, cursing and screaming, with excrement all over his head.

A devout lay Buddhist saw that enraged man approaching and calmly inquired what had happened. Having been told that a bucket of filth had been thrown over him by one of those @#*%! nuns, the lay Buddhist exclaimed: "Awesome! You are so lucky! To receive a personal blessing from a holy nun in such a unique way is mega auspicious."

"Really?" said the gullible businessman.

"Absolutely! Now go home, shower, and get changed, then go to the palace. Something wonderful will happen to you today."

The businessman rushed back home, having no time to spare to burn down the nun's monastery, washed, changed, and went to the palace. That morning, the king gave the businessman a very lucrative government contract.

The delighted businessman told all his friends, "If you want real good luck in your business, ask the holy nuns for the most auspicious of all blessings—holy shit. It worked for me!"

When the Buddha heard this story doing the rounds, he admonished the nuns. He told them that they were extremely lucky that day to have a quick-thinking layperson who convinced that superstitious businessman that having filth poured over your head is auspicious. Some people will believe anything.

As a result, the Buddha established a monastic rule for the nuns. For the past 2,500 years, the eighth rule for Buddhist nuns in the section called Pacittiya is: "A nun must not throw shit over the monastery wall."

42. The Origin of Materialism

A good nun lived a very simple life, with few possessions and dwelling in a cave. Every morning, she would take her alms bowl to the nearby village to collect just enough food for her one meal of the day. She had plenty of time to meditate, study, and teach what she knew to any of the local villagers.

When she returned from almsround one morning, she noticed a hole in her spare robe, so she found a small piece of cloth and hand sewed a patch onto the robe. She'd done this before. You see, in her cave lived a family of mice, and they liked nibbling her robes. While sewing, she thought that if she had a cat, then there would be no mice, and she wouldn't have to spend so much time sewing patches. So the next day, she asked the villagers for a cat, and they gave her a well-behaved brown cat whose color matched her robes.

The cat needed milk and fish, so the nun had to ask the villagers for these extra items every morning. One morning, she thought that if she had her own cow, then she wouldn't need to keep asking for milk to feed the cat to keep away the mice that chewed her robes. So she asked one of her wealthy supporters for a cow.

Once the nun had a cow, she had to get grass for the cow to eat. So she begged the villagers for grass to feed her cow to provide milk for the cat to keep away the mice that chewed her robes.

After a few days, the nun thought that if she had her own field, then she would not need to harass the poor villagers for grass every day. So she arranged for a collection to be made to buy a nearby pasture to provide grass for her cow to provide milk for the cat to keep away the mice that chewed her robes.

It was a lot of work looking after the pasture, catching the cow every morning and milking it, so she thought that it would be helpful to have a boy, a young attendant who could do all these chores for her. In return, the nun would give him moral guidance and teachings. The villagers selected a boy from a poor family in dire need of some moral guidance. Now she had a boy to look after the pasture to provide grass for her cow to provide milk for the cat to keep away the mice that chewed her robes.

Now the nun needed to collect more than twice as much food every morning, because young boys eat a lot. Moreover, she needed a small hut nearby for the boy to sleep in, because it was against the rules for the boy to sleep in the cave with a nun. So she asked the villagers to build a hut for her boy who looked after the pasture to provide grass for her cow to provide milk for the cat to keep away the mice that chewed her robes.

By this time, she began to notice the villagers avoiding her. They were afraid that she was going to ask them for something more. Even when they saw a brown cow approaching in the distance, thinking it was the nun, they would run away or hide in their houses with the door securely bolted and the curtains drawn over the windows.

When a villager did come to ask her some questions on meditation, she said, "Sorry. Not now. I'm too busy. I have to check the hut being built for the boy who looks after my field to graze my cow that provides the milk for my brown cat that keeps away the mice so that I don't need to keep patching my robe."

She noticed what she was saying and realized: "Such is the origin of materialism."

She then told the villagers to dismantle the hut, sent the boy back to his family, gave away the cow and the field, and found a good home for her cat.

A few days later, she had returned to her simple life, with few possessions and dwelling in a cave. After returning one morning from the village with just enough alms food for her one meal of the day, she noticed that a mouse had chewed another hole in her robe.

With a quiet smile, she sewed on another patch.

43. Kit-Cat

This is a true story of a remarkable cat that lived in Bodhinyana Monastery, sixty-five kilometers south of Perth, where I live.

Kit-Cat was born in my monastery, her mother being a feral cat that lived in the adjacent state forest. We discovered her as an abandoned and hungry little kitten, sheltering in a hollow log.

As Kit-Cat grew, she started to catch small birds. We tried hanging a bell around her neck, but this only succeeded in training her to move with more stealth, so the bell made no sound. Although the monks loved little Kit-Cat, she was catching more poor birds, so sadly we realized she had to go. An Australian forest is not the right environment for a domestic cat.

I found a nice home for Kit-Cat in the oceanside suburb of Watermans Bay to the north of Perth. On the day that Kit-Cat left, I picked her up, put her in a sack, and placed her in the back of her new owner's car, in the place where your feet usually go. I felt guilty doing this to a cat that had trusted me.

Chris, the new owner, drove the cat straight to her home in Watermans Bay, took the sack inside her house, and only released Kit-Cat after all the doors had been closed. She wanted Kit-Cat to get accustomed to her new family before letting her out into the garden.

Three days later, on a hot Saturday afternoon, she let Kit-Cat into the garden. Immediately, Kit-Cat ran for the garden gate, and Chris tried to stop her, but the cat was too fast. Kit-Cat leapt over the gate and out into the street. Chris got into her car and drove around the neighborhood looking for Kit-Cat but found no trace. Kit-Cat had disappeared.

At this point, you are probably thinking that Kit-Cat eventually found her way back home to my monastery, eighty-five kilometers away. If so, you are wrong. Kit-cat was far too smart to walk such a long distance.

That Saturday I was on teaching duty in our city center located in Nollamara, seventy-eight kilometers north of my monastery and around twelve kilometers southeast of Watermans Bay. While passing by the thick, closed wooden door of our Perth temple, I heard a strange noise outside. When I opened the door, there was little Kit-Cat looking up at me and mewing. As I cradled her to bring her inside, I noticed that her paws were burning hot. It was over forty degrees Celsius (105° Fahrenheit!) outside that day. I gave her saucer after saucer of milk, she was so dehydrated. Then I let her do what cats do best, curl up and rest.

Soon after Kit-Cat arrived, I received a phone call from a very apologetic Chris. "I'm so sorry, Ajahn Brahm. I let your cat out and it bolted. I've been driving around looking for her for almost two hours. I'm so sorry. Maybe she'll find her way back to your monastery in Serpentine."

"No worries, Chris," I replied. "Kit-Cat is here with me in Nollamara."

I remember Chris gasping. She couldn't believe it. She later came to check for herself. Kit-Cat had found me in a big city she had never been to before. She had run at least twelve kilometres in just under two hours, crossing a major motorway and other busy roads, with no maps and unable to ask for directions, to the one person who cared for her in a city of over a million.

Kit-Cat had only left our monastery once, to go to the local vet to be "monasticized" so she wouldn't have any kittens. She had never been close to the sprawling Perth metropolitan area before; she was a country cat. When she left my monastery, it was in a sack on the floor in the back seat. There was no way she could have seen where she was going. Yet the clever cat found me!

Of course, after that Kit-Cat came back to my monastery, where she lived many happy years. After twenty-two years of cat life, she died there and is buried under the holy bodhi tree by our main hall.

44. A Dog's Retreat

To be fair to all pets, I now relate a story that was sent to me recently about how a very smart dog dealt with the stress of modern life.

A woman returning from a shopping trip opened the door of her suburban house. Suddenly, out of nowhere, a big dog rushed past her into her house. By the time the woman had put her bags down, the dog was curled up in a corner of a quiet room, fast asleep. The dog was a Labrador, had a collar on, and was well groomed, so it was certainly not a stray. The kind woman liked dogs, especially this one, so she let it stay. After about two hours, the dog woke up and the woman let it out. The dog then disappeared.

The next day, the dog returned to her house, and she let it come inside again. The dog went to the same quiet corner, curled up, and went to sleep for another two hours.

After this same pattern repeated two or three more times, the woman began to wonder where this lovable dog lived and why it kept coming back to her house. So she wrote a note, folded it, and placed it under the Labrador's collar. The note said something like:

> Your dog has been coming to my house every afternoon
> for the past five days. All it does is sleep quietly. It is such
> a lovely, good-natured dog that I don't mind. I just wonder
> where it lives and why it keeps coming.

The next day the dog returned to sleep in its corner, but with another note tucked into the collar. The reply read:

> My dog lives in a noisy house with my nagging wife and four children, two of whom are under five. He comes to your house for some peace and quiet and to catch up on his sleep. May I come too?

45. An Amazing Tale of the Supernatural

An Australian man was on a group trek in the foothills of the Himalayas, in the region to the west of Tibet called Ladakh. The scenery was so spectacular that he lingered behind the others taking photo after photo. Thinking to catch up with the rest of the group by taking a shortcut, he unfortunately took a wrong path, lost sight of the others, and became completely lost.

After wandering in the wilderness without a map for a couple of hours, he became anxious. The sun had set behind the peaks, it was getting darker and colder by the minute, and he was still completely lost. This was getting dangerous.

In the distance, he saw the faint glow of lights. Walking toward them, he made out an old Buddhist monastery, secluded on the mountain. Approaching, he rapped on the large wooden door framing the entrance to the temple. After some time he heard the shuffle of footsteps, and the door creaked open to reveal a small, frail old monk, the abbot of the monastery.

The kind abbot listened to his story and invited him to stay the night in his own quarters, the only room in the monastery with a Western-style bed. The compassionate abbot would sleep elsewhere. He knew where the trekkers went and would give him a young monk the following day to guide him back to his trekking group.

After a simple supper, the exhausted Australian quickly fell asleep in the abbot's comfortable bed. Just after midnight, he woke up to the sound of the most amazing music he had ever heard. He had attended many concerts at the Sydney Opera House, but never, never had he listened to such a soft yet thrilling melody and felt such bliss. Tears rolled down his cheeks in ecstasy as he lay in bed soaking up every divine note. He did not know when, but the heavenly music took him into the most relaxing deep sleep of his life. He woke up fully rested and content for the first time in many years.

After breakfast, he went to thank the abbot for lending him his bed. He also told the abbot about the music and asked what it was.

"Oh, that," said the abbot.

"Yes, it was incredible. I've never heard anything like it."

"That, young man, is something supernatural. According to our monastery rules, I cannot tell you because you are not a monk."

The Australian frowned, got out his wallet, and offered the abbot a hundred dollars.

"No, no." said the abbot.

"Okay, how much?" asked the Australian.

"Look," replied the abbot firmly, "even if you offered 100 million dollars, I still couldn't tell you. Only monks may know!"

The Australian could not bribe the abbot, and so he left. Soon, he rejoined his group, successfully completed the trek, and returned to Australia.

Back home, he kept thinking about that supernatural music. He started obsessing so much about it that he began to lose sleep and became distracted at work. He saw one of the best psychologists in Sydney, but still he could not get that music out of his head. It was literally driving him crazy. There was only one thing to do.

Almost a year to the day since his previous visit, he appeared at the gate of that monastery in Ladakh and asked to see the abbot. The abbot remembered him. The Australian explained that he simply had to find out what made that music; otherwise he would go mad.

"I'm so sorry," said the abbot with genuine compassion. "As I told you the last time, I cannot tell you because you are not a monk."

"So make me a monk!" replied the Australian.

It takes two years of training, study, and learning all the chants to become a monk in a strict monastery. The Australian put himself through all that rigorous process, and finally after two years, the abbot ordained him as a monk.

As soon as the ordination was over, the Australian asked the abbot, "Now I am a monk, you can tell me. What is that heavenly music?"

Smiling, the abbot replied, "Come to my room at midnight and I will show you."

The new monk was there one hour early, such was his excitement. He had waited three years and sacrificed everything, training hard to become a monk. The moment had now arrived.

Just before midnight, the abbot took out an old set of keys from his desk and drew back a curtain in his room to reveal a hidden wooden door. The abbot opened that door with a key made from wood. The labored creak of the door told that it had not been opened for many years, maybe even decades. There was a corridor, at the end of which was another door made of iron. As they walked toward it, an old clock in the monastery sounded the twelve chimes of midnight. The abbot used an iron key to open the second heavy door. After they had walked through, the heavenly music started. Being much closer, it was clear and sweet. Waves of joy swept through the Australian's body. Nothing in his life meant anything compared to this. They walked toward another door, and the abbot took out his silver key, for this door was made of solid silver mined from the mountains. It would be worth a fortune in Australia, but you don't think of such things when you are hearing music whose beauty is beyond words. After opening the silver door, he could see what was obviously the final door. It was made of pure gold, six inches thick, and decorated with priceless gems. The abbot took out a large golden key and then paused in front of the gold door. Turning to the Australian, he said with a gravity that demands one's full attention, "Are you sure you're ready for this? It's something supernatural. It will change you forever. Are you prepared for that?"

The Australian was excited and terrified at the same time. He had never made such a momentous decision before. Seeing what was behind the gold door might send him mad, but not seeing it would drive him crazy. So he said, "Okay. Let's do it."

The abbot placed the key in the lock. The Australian's body began to shake as the abbot slowly opened the heavy, ancient gold door.

And there it was! Oh my Lord! It was too much for any mere mortal to comprehend! It went beyond this world! It transcended all perceptions!

And what was it?

I am sorry, but I am not allowed to tell you, because you're not a monk!

46. My Own Himalayan Journey

I saw my first pictures of the Himalayas while I was at school in London. They were so vast, so wild and alluring, that I decided that I would go there myself one day.

During the northern summer of 1973, after finishing university and before starting work as a schoolteacher, I set off from Victoria Station in London for India and the mighty Himalaya. Two weeks later I was in India, and it was raining every day. If I had checked before planning my journey, I would have discovered that this was monsoon season on the subcontinent. Even going as far north as Kathmandu, I could see only rain clouds, never the Himalayas. I soon gave up any hope of seeing the greatest mountains in the world. Fortunately, there were many other things to do in such an exotic land.

One day in Kathmandu, a couple of Americans told me that there was a vehicle carrying the mail going north to the border with Tibet and it took travelers along for a few rupees. It was an attractive outing, so early the next morning, I was on the mail van going north.

Around 1:00, the driver of the van stopped for lunch in a little mountain village. The two Americans suggested we climb a small hill close by while our driver had his meal. Fifteen minutes later, when we reached the top of the hill, the clouds to the north parted. For the first time, I could see the vast range of the Himalaya in the rain-cleansed air. The view was more breathtaking than the climb up that hill.

Wanting to take a picture, I realized I had left my camera in the mail van, so I quickly ran down the hill, gathered the camera, and scampered up the hill as fast as I could. Just as I reached the summit, the clouds closed. I had missed out by only a few seconds. As it would turn out, I wouldn't see the mountains again. The Americans, who had simply sat enjoying the inspiring view, turned to me to ask where I had gone. Even worse, they then described to me in awestruck detail the amazing view and wonder that I had lost.

I felt such a dummy. Fetching my camera had cost me the extraordinary view. But I learned that when you try to capture a moment, with a photograph or by noting it down, it often escapes from you, and you miss all the wonder.

Like the glorious Himalaya, our life's magic moments are for experiencing and not for imprisoning in a camera. They are unforgettable anyway, so why do we need to photograph them?

47. someone is watching you

In the ancient world, a single wise teacher would teach a group of students everything they needed to know about life. One such teacher had a dozen students who were close to graduation. He also had a daughter who all his students thought was hot.

One day he announced to his students that he had two problems. The first was that he had to find a husband for his daughter, and according to the tradition of those days, it should be one of his twelve students. The difficulty was that he couldn't decide which student would make the best husband.

The second problem was that he, as the father of the bride, would have to pay for a lavish wedding ceremony and also set up the couple in a new house with all the necessities. The difficulty was that this was a great expense.

To solve both these problems, the teacher announced a contest. He asked his students to creep stealthily into the local village under the cover of night and steal whatever they could, as long as no one saw them. Then they would bring all the goods back to the teacher. Whichever student followed the instructions and stole the most would win his daughter, and all the stolen valuables would go to the happy couple.

The students were shocked that their teacher was asking them to steal. He was usually such a moral man. In those days, though, so important was the vow of obedience to one's teacher that they accepted the contest. Or perhaps it was that all the young men were blinded by desire for their teacher's gorgeous daughter?

Over the next seven days, the cunning students snuck into the village late at night, stole whatever they could, and brought it back to their teacher. The teacher kept a careful record of which student stole what and from which house. Amazingly, no student got caught in the act.

At the end of the week, the teacher assembled the students to announce the result.

"You have stolen so much," began the teacher, "enough for any couple to get a good start in life. Except for one of you, who has not brought back anything at all. Why not?"

The shy young student came forward and said, "Because I had to follow your instructions, sir."

"What do you mean? Did I not instruct you to steal and bring the goods back to me?"

"Yes, sir," said the student, with downcast eyes, "but you also instructed us to steal *as long as no one sees you*. I crept into many houses at 2:00 in the morning, when everyone was fast asleep. But every time I was about to steal something, I noticed someone was watching me. So I had to leave empty-handed, sir."

"If everyone in the house was sleeping, then who was watching you?" asked the teacher.

"I was watching me, sir. I could see myself about to steal. That is why I took nothing."

"Very good! Very good!" exclaimed the delighted teacher. "At least I have one wise student who has been listening to me all these years. All the rest of you nincompoops, take all the stolen goods back to their owners. They won't punish you. I told them about this 'contest' two weeks ago. They were expecting you. That is why none of you were caught. And remember, whatever immoral act you do, someone will always see you, and that someone is yourself. Because you see it, you will feel bad and suffer."

Of course, the wise student married the beautiful daughter. The teacher was wealthy enough to give them an opulent wedding ceremony and a well-furnished dream house. Then, because the husband was truly wise, they actually did live happily ever after.

48. How Another Student Learned to Laugh at Abuse

The former story was from ancient India. The following story is from ancient Greece, where the method of education was very similar. A single teacher would teach his students everything.

One particular teacher was bad tempered and would often scold a student for making the slightest mistake. Having verbally abused the young man, the teacher would then charge him for the privilege of being admonished. It was regarded as an extra tutorial, worthy of a fee to the teacher.

One such student went to work in Athens after graduating. Whenever his boss or anyone else verbally abused him, the student would laugh merrily.

In those days, one of the worst curses, coming from the nearby Middle East, was: "May the fleas from a thousand camels infest your armpits!"

He even laughed at that. He did not get upset at any insult. His friends and colleagues thought he was a few pillars short of a Greek temple, but in all other matters he appeared sane. So they asked him why he always laughed when he was rebuked.

"When I was a student," he replied, "I had to pay for being criticized. Now I get it for free. That is what makes me so happy."

Perhaps we should charge our children every time we have to shout at them for not cleaning their room or for not doing their homework. Then, later on in their lives, when their partner scolds them or a boss shouts at them, they will never get angry and only laugh merrily, like that student of ancient Greece.

49. Learning from the Experts

My Christian friends at Cambridge told me that they were about to do some volunteer work at the local hospital for those with mental disabilities. As a Buddhist, I thought that I should volunteer too—to "keep up with the Joneses" as they say. So my reason for going was nothing more than religious pride.

Every Thursday afternoon, we would catch the bus from Cambridge to Fulbourn Hospital to help in the occupational therapy department for those institutionalized with Down's syndrome. My Christian friends stopped going after a few weeks, but I carried on for two years. Even though my studies in theoretical physics took up most of my spare time (after my busy social life, which took priority of course), I never missed the chance to go to visit my friends with Down's syndrome. I truly enjoyed every Thursday afternoon.

What surprised me was how emotionally intelligent they were. If I arrived tired after last night's party, or depressed after breaking up with a girlfriend, they would pick it up straight away. They would give me a hug and a sincere smile that would melt me. Their hearts were open and uncomplicated, not like mine!

It was awkward for me, as a heterosexual in the early seventies, being embraced in public by another man so affectionately. But the innocent joy that I saw all over my friend's face while hugging me taught me to relax and enjoy it too. Life was uncomplicated at Fulbourn Hospital, among people who understood the emotional world so well. It was so different from studying in Cambridge University among those who were experts in everything except their own feelings.

I was so experienced after two years at Fulbourn Hospital that one Thursday the head of the OT department assigned me to one group all by myself for the first part of the afternoon and another group for the second part of the afternoon, again by myself. I never suspected a thing. Those friends with Down's syndrome sure could keep a secret.

As I was about to leave, the real OT staff, the ones who were paid, called me into the big room. There stood all my friends with Down's syndrome grinning like their faces would split, together with the staff. They were to make a presentation to me as the longest volunteering student that they had ever had.

While I had been working with one group, the other group and the staff were busy making presents for me. Now they were to make the presentation.

The gifts were not refined enough to sell in any shop, but they made me cry. By now, I had learned from my Down's syndrome teachers how to let the tears flow in public. It was delightful. The head of the OT department said she had realized that my final examinations were to begin next week and that this would be my last day, hence the wonderful ceremony of gratitude. I replied through my tears that, actually, my exams did not start for another ten days. "May I come back next week, please?" They kindly allowed me an extra week.

Looking back, I learned most of what is now called "emotional intelligence" from those friends with Down's syndrome. To this day, I regard them as the experts, my teachers.

50. Giving overcomes Depression

Those who do voluntary community work often begin with the idea that they are giving something back to society. However, they usually finish up realizing that they have received much more than they ever gave. Their experience tells them that giving your time to a good cause is not an expense but an investment, always with a high rate of return.

I often counsel people with depression to go find some old people's home, some hospital or other charity, and volunteer their time. Giving to others adds meaning to their lives. In voluntary service they find what they have lost: their meaning.

When giving service we receive nutritious emotional feedback, like I received serving my friends with Down's syndrome. We are helped by those we thought we were helping. Our self-esteem rises, and we actually begin to like ourselves and our life. That is the end of our depression.

It may also make one rich, as the following story shows.

A friend had recently moved into a small apartment as a result of a divorce. He was unable to keep his pedigree dog in such cramped accommodation but was able to find a good home for her with a kind elderly woman who had another dog of the same breed.

One day, the elderly woman called him at work to ask if he would be able to drive her from her suburban home to the doctor in the city for an appointment. She was desperate and could not find any other means of transport.

My friend was running a one-man advertising business at the time that was just getting by. Being his own boss, he was able to take the time off to drive the woman to her appointment. That began a regular private taxi service for the dear old woman. My friend didn't mind taking her to the dentist or wherever, because he got joy out of helping her and it was a welcome break from the grind of his work.

One morning she called to ask if he were free to take her to an important appointment with her lawyer. He obliged, as usual, and dropped her outside her lawyer's offices in town. She asked politely if he could spare a few more moments to accompany her inside, which he happily did. There, in front of her lawyer, to his astonishment, she made him the sole beneficiary of her estate, which was substantial. The elderly woman was to die soon after.

My friend was amazed at his good fortune. He was only being kind and, anyway, he enjoyed looking after her. The last thing that he expected was to inherit such wealth. But that is what happens when we volunteer our time to help others. At the very least we feel good about ourselves, and sometimes there are other surprises too!

51. The Deep Hole

A man was walking through a forest when he spotted a hole. He stopped to look in and saw a large bag of gold at the bottom. He reached in to grab the treasure, but the hole was too deep. No matter how hard he stretched, he could not reach the gold. So he gave up.

As he continued his walk through the forest, he met another man and told him about the gold in the hole that was too deep to reach. The second man picked up a hooked stick, went to the hole, and pulled out the gold using the stick.

The problem was not that the hole was too deep, but that the first man's arm was too short. The second man increased the length of his arm with a hooked stick, and he could easily reach the treasure.

Happiness is never too far to reach. We just need to increase our wisdom and compassion.

Then we can reach anything.

52. When Is It Okay to Lie?

An elderly Buddhist woman called me one evening in great distress. She told me that that afternoon she had lied to her husband for the first time since they had been married forty years ago. She said she felt terrible.

Her husband, Don, had had a heart attack and survived. However, he urgently needed bypass surgery and so was put in a hospital ward to wait until he was strong enough.

There were three other male patients in the same room, also waiting for a bypass. Don became quite friendly with Jack in the adjacent bed. So much so that, when Don's wife visited one evening, he asked how Jack was doing after his bypass operation that had been done that morning.

"Oh, Jack's fine," said his wife. "He is recovering in the ICU."

The truth was that Don's wife had just met Jack's grieving family in the hospital's foyer. Jack had died. She could not bear to tell her husband that his new friend had died from the same operation that he was to have the following day. So she lied.

Don only just survived his own bypass operation. He was on the edge of life and death for three days, but he pulled through. I often think that if his wife had told him the truth, the extra worry would probably have been enough to push him over that edge into death. The lie had saved his life.

So I tell my followers that it is okay to lie sometimes. But only once every forty years!

53. why we Lie

"Don't you realize," said the judge to the defendant in the murder trial, "that the penalty for perjury is very severe?"

"Yes," replied the accused, "but it is far less than the penalty for murder!"

This explains why people lie so much: the penalty is usually far less when you lie than it is when you tell the truth.

For instance, a few years ago, a young girl came to me because she had become pregnant by her boyfriend.

"Why don't you tell your mum and dad?" I asked.

"Are you kidding?" she replied. "They would kill me!"

So she lied to her parents instead.

It would be a far happier and healthier world if the value of honesty were raised so high that the penalty when you tell the truth is *always* far less than when you lie. The only way to achieve this is by giving amnesty, no matter for what, as long as the truth is told.

Then sons or daughters could tell their parents even the most embarrassing things, knowing that they would never be punished, not even scolded, but helped. When children are in big trouble, this is the time that they need their parents the most. Usually, they are too scared to confide and get help. Also, married couples could be totally honest with each other, working through any marital difficulties together instead of concealing them.

To all parents reading this book, please tell your kids that whatever it is that they have done, when they tell you the truth then they will never be punished or lectured but only receive help and understanding.

To all couples, promise each other that honesty is regarded as more precious than anything else in your relationship, so that there will never be any punishment, even for unfaithful behavior, but a forgiveness of each other's weaknesses and a commitment to work together to make sure they do not reoccur.

Having promised them this, then keep the promise.

> *Where there are punishments, even scolding, the truth will be hidden.*

That is why we don't do punishments in Buddhism.

After the apartheid years in South Africa, it took the moral courage and wisdom of leaders such as Nelson Mandela and Archbishop Tutu to establish the first Truth and Reconciliation Commission. They understood that uncovering the truth of what happened in those brutal years was more important than punishment.

One incident from the Truth and Reconciliation Commission that continues to inspire me was when a white police officer confessed, in detail, how he had tortured and killed a black political activist. The testimony was being given in front of the tortured activist's widow.

Her husband had been one of the many who had disappeared. Now, for the first time, she was hearing what had happened to the man that she had chosen to love above all others, the father of her children.

The police officer was trembling and weeping with overwhelming guilt as he forced himself to reveal the vicious cruelty of what he had done. When the confession was over, the widow leaped over the barrier meant to protect the witnesses and ran straight for her husband's murderer. The guards were too stunned to stop her.

The guilty police officer expected violent revenge at the hands of the widow and would accept it. But she never attacked him. Instead, she wrapped her strong black arms gently around the passive white body of her husband's murderer and said, "I forgive you." The two of them stood there in the embrace of reconciliation.

All who were there broke out in tears. They wept, for a long time. Forgiving the unforgiveable shone hope into their future. In that moment, through their wet eyes, they could glimpse the possibility of racial harmony, and the end of fear, in that land.

If the brutal torture and extrajudicial murder of the one you love the most can be forgiven, what is left that cannot be forgiven?

When there is forgiveness, only then will there be truth.

54. Monkey Minds

A monkey was visiting a Buddhist monastery on one of the holy days. He thought that there would be so many visitors bringing offerings of food that someone was sure to drop a mango, or leave an apple unattended, and that would be his lunch.

As he was loitering outside the monastery's big hall, he happened to hear an old monk give a sermon about the "monkey mind." Thinking that this might be of interest to a monkey, the monkey listened.

"The monkey mind," taught the old monk, "is a restless mind, always jumping from one thing to another, like a monkey jumping from one branch to another in the jungle. It is a bad mind that needs to be rectified through the practice of meditation in order to find peace."

When the monkey heard the monkey mind being called a bad mind, he became angry. "What do they mean a monkey mind is bad! I am a monkey and monkey minds are just fine. These humans are slandering us. This is unfair. This is not right. I have to do something about this gross defamation!" Then the monkey swung through the trees back to his home deep in the forest to complain to his friends.

Soon, the large troop of monkeys was jumping up and down squealing, "They can't get away with slandering us! This is species discrimination! How dare they! Let's get a lawyer from the World Wildlife Fund. We monkeys have rights too!"

"Stop it!" ordered the leader of the troop. "Don't you see? That monk was right. Look at yourselves, jumping up and down making so much noise. That is the result of having a monkey mind. You monkeys just can't be still."

The monkeys realized that their leader was correct. They were all cursed with monkey minds and would never find any peace. They all hung their heads and brooded in sullen silence.

"Hey!" said the monkey who had been to the temple. "I've got an idea. I heard that monk teach that if you meditate, then you can overcome the monkey mind and find peace."

The happy monkeys started jumping up and down again, squealing, "Yeah! Cool! Let's meditate. Let's find peace of mind."

After much jumping about, one monkey asked, "So how do we meditate?"

"First we have to find a cushion to sit on," said one monkey.

"Yeah! Cool! Let's find cushions!" And after a lot more jumping around and shrieking, they went off into the forest and collected a lot of grass and soft leaves which they fashioned into *zafus*, the Buddhist name for a meditation cushion.

"What do we do next?"

"Sit on the cushion," said the monkey who visited the temple. "Cross your legs and place your right paw over the left paw, with thumbs slightly touching. Keep your back straight. Close your eyes and observe your breathing."

This was the first time in history that monkeys meditated. The forest had never been so quiet. Unfortunately, it did not last long.

"Excuse me! Excuse me!" interrupted one monkey, and all the others opened their eyes. "I've been thinking. Don't you all remember that we had planned to raid the banana plantation for our lunch today? I can't stop thinking about it. So why don't we all raid the banana plantation first, get that out of the way, and then we will meditate?"

"Yeah! Cool! Great idea!" shouted the other monkeys, jumping up and down again, and off they went to raid the plantation.

They stole many bananas, heaped them up in a pile, and having got that out of the way, went back to their meditation cushions. They sat down, crossed their legs, placed the right paw carefully over the left paw, straightened their backs, closed their eyes, and resumed meditating.

After two more minutes, another monkey put up her hand. "Excuse me! Excuse me! I've been thinking too. Before we eat those bananas, we have to peel them first. Let's get that out of the way, and then I can meditate without thinking about it."

"Yeah! Cool! We've been thinking the same!" screamed the other monkeys. So once again the monkeys were jumping up and down, shrieking, and peeling all the bananas.

Having peeled them all and placed them in a heap, the monkeys went back to their cushions. Once again, they sat down, crossed their legs, placed the right paw carefully over the left paw, straightened their backs, closed their eyes, and observed the natural flow of their breathing.

"Excuse me! Excuse me!" screeched yet another monkey after only a minute. "I've been thinking also. Before we eat those bananas, we have to place them in our mouths. Let's get that out of the way first, and then we can meditate peacefully without having to think."

"Yeah! Cool! What a brilliant idea!" And all the monkeys jumped up and down, making a lot of noise, and put a banana in their mouths. A few monkeys put two bananas in their mouth, and one put in three. Some monkeys are no different than some people. But they did not eat them yet. This was just to get something out of the way so they didn't have to think about it and could be free to meditate instead.

They sat down on their cushions again, crossed their legs, placed the right paw carefully over the left paw, straightened their backs, closed their eyes, and resumed meditating with bananas in their mouths.

Of course, once all eyes were closed, the monkeys ate all their bananas, got up, and left. That was the end of their one-and-only meditation session.

Now you know why we humans have difficulty finding peace of mind. Most of us have monkey minds, which say:

> I will just get this one thing out of the way first, and then I'll rest.

That is why, as I mentioned in my previous book, the only place these days that you find people "resting in peace" is in the cemetery. And in the Buddhist monastery, of course!

55. Let Go of the Banana

In ancient times, it was easy to capture a monkey. The hunter would wander into a forest, find a ripe coconut, and cut out a small hole that was exactly the same size as a monkey's fist. He would then drink the sweet milk and eat some of the soft flesh.

Having eaten, he would secure the empty coconut to a tree with a thick rope or leather strap. After placing a banana inside the coconut, the hunter would go home.

Sure enough, a monkey would discover that hollow coconut with a banana inside and try to pull it out. But the hole is only just big enough for a monkey to put in an empty fist. When his fist was holding the banana, he couldn't get it out.

By the time the hunter returns, the monkey has been struggling for hours to get his fist out together with the banana. Seeing the hunter, the monkey tries even harder to get both his fist and the banana out.

All the monkey needs to do to escape is to let go of the banana. Then he can pull his hand out and run. But does the monkey let go?

No way! Because monkeys always think, "It is *my* banana. I found it. It's mine!"

And that is how monkeys get captured every time.

It's also how humans get captured.

Say your dear son dies and you can't stop grieving over him. You think about him all the time. You can't sleep or work. Why?

All you need to do is to "let go of the banana" and you can move on in your life without suffering so much.

But you can't let go. Only because you think, "It's *my* son. I gave birth to him. He's mine."

Mothers tell me that when they look into the eyes of their newborn child for the first time, they intuitively know that this is a being not totally made from the parents; it is a being with its own past and individuality, a visitor from somewhere unknown who has now entered their life. It is theirs to care for, nurture, and love . . . not to possess.

Unfortunately, many parents forget this over the years and start owning their children. So when it is time to let them go, they can't. If only they had remembered that one person can never own another, not even one's own child. Then they would never get captured like a monkey and suffer with grief.

To love someone is to one day let them go.

56. Mummy, I'm Leaving Home

We often fear that if we let someone go, they will never come back. The opposite is often the case.

If you keep a bird locked in a cage, then one day, when you leave the cage door open by accident, the bird will fly away and never return.

Alternatively, if you keep the cage door open, ensuring that the cage is comfortable with a plentiful supply of good food, then the bird will fly away but always come back.

A young Australian Buddhist mother told me that her six-year-old son was so upset one afternoon that he pronounced in all seriousness, "Mummy, I don't love you anymore, and I am leaving home!"

"Okay darling. I'll help you pack," the mother replied.

So she accompanied her little boy into his bedroom and helped him pack all the essentials, like his teddy bear, lucky pants, and Spiderman costume, into his little suitcase. Having packed the suitcase, mum went into the kitchen and made her son's favorite sandwiches, placed them in a brown paper bag, and gave them to her six-year-old so he would not go hungry when he left home.

Standing at the open front door of their house, the mother waved her son goodbye, "Bye-bye, darling! Don't forget to keep in touch!" The young child, carrying a suitcase in one hand and the sandwiches in the other hand, walked to the end of the short garden path, opened the gate, turned left, and walked off into his future.

Less than fifty metres later, the six-year-old was homesick. He turned around, walked back to the gate, and ran the short distance to the door of his home and into the welcoming arms of his mother, who hadn't moved.

That was a very wise mum. She knew her little six-year-old wouldn't go far from a loving home.

When I told that story to a psychologist from Singapore, she couldn't stop laughing. After she had pulled herself together, she explained that almost the same thing had happened to her when she was a very young girl. She had an argument with her mother when she was six and demanded to leave home. Her mum immediately agreed and helped pack her bag. This young girl didn't receive any sandwiches, however. Her mum gave her ten Singapore dollars to buy her own lunch! Her mum then accompanied her to the elevator, as they lived in an apartment block. The elevator arrived; the six-year-old girl stepped in, and the mother waved her goodbye as the elevator doors closed.

This young girl did not even make it outside the elevator before she became homesick. By the time the lift had reached the ground floor, she missed her mummy and her home terribly. She pressed the button for the floor on which she lived. When the elevator doors opened, mum was standing there with open arms. "Welcome home, darling!"

When the bonds of love are strong, you can let people go, knowing with certainty they will come back.

57. Passing over the Horizon

In the days before reliable aircraft, most people would travel from continent to continent on huge, ocean-going passenger liners. When the ship was about to cast off, the passengers would line the ship's decks next to the pier, on which their relatives and friends stood. As the steam horn sounded the departure, both waved, blew kisses, and shouted their last goodbyes as the ship slowly moved away. Soon, the boat was too far away for those on the pier to distinguish who was who in the grey mass of passengers still standing on the decks, but still they would wave and gaze. A few minutes later, the loved ones still remained on the pier, staring at the ever-diminishing ship, somewhere in which was their loved one.

Then the boat would reach that defining line, the horizon, and disappear totally. Yet even though the relatives and friends on dry land could not see their loved one anymore, let alone speak with them or touch them, they knew that they had not disappeared totally. They had just gone over a line, the horizon, that separates us from what is beyond. They know that they will see them again.

The same can be said to happen when our loved ones die. If we are lucky, we are by their bedside, embracing them and saying our last goodbyes. Then they sail off into the ocean that is death. They fade away from us. At their last, they reach the horizon, the defining line that separates this life from what is beyond. After they have passed that line, we cannot see them anymore, let alone speak to them or touch them, but we know that they have not totally disappeared. They have just gone over a line, death, which separates us from what is beyond.

We will see each other again.

58. The Frightened Water Buffalo

Water buffaloes in old Thailand were part of the family. They would live in the space below a villager's house. They were usually so docile that little kids could safely go to sleep on their backs while the buffalo grazed lazily in the warm, idle months of the Thai hot season.

Sometimes, though, a water buffalo would take fright for reasons only known to itself. Raising its head with a snort, it would charge off in any direction.

A local villager was taking his water buffalo to his fields to graze early one morning, and as he was passing our forest monastery, something in the jungle spooked the buffalo. The buffalo raised his head and snorted. The villager tried to hold him back with the thin rope tied loosely around the buffalo's neck, but the rope quickly wound around the villager's finger, and as the buffalo charged off, it took the top of the man's finger with it!

The poor man came directly into our monastery for help, with his hand covered in blood and half a finger missing. We took him to the hospital and had him patched up. He soon recovered.

I often use that unfortunate tale as an example of what happens when we don't let go.

Who is stronger, a man or a water buffalo?

It doesn't make sense to hold on to a water buffalo when it's charging. Let it go. The buffalo only runs off a few hundred meters and then stops by itself. Then the farmer can calmly walk after it, take hold of the rope again, and lead it to the fields to graze.

Too many people hold back what they should let go, and they lose many fingers.

59. The Case of the Disappearing Harley

One of the first residents at my monastery was Patrick. He was a spiritual man with no family and no fixed address. He used to travel from one monastery to another, from one spiritual community to the next. He was a temple hopper. Thus it was that he came to stay at my monastery in the early years to help with the hard physical work of building the basic facilities.

He had no house or savings. The only thing of value that he possessed was a magnificent Harley Davidson motorbike that he was very pleased with. It allowed him to travel around Australia, enjoying the freedom of being without ties to any person or place.

He wrote to me regarding his experience in a large shopping mall in Sydney. After parking his Harley in the multi-story parking lot, he purchased a few items and returned to his bike. To his shock, the parking bay was empty. Someone had stolen his Harley!

That precious bike was the only thing of value that he owned. He had saved up so long to buy it. It was the machine that gave him the freedom to roam wherever he will. Now it had been taken by some lowlife. Now he had nothing.

He'd been listening to Buddhist teachings long enough to know the meaning of attachment. He remembered the Buddha's advice that:

All that is mine, beloved and pleasing,
will one day become separated from me.

Thus he quickly came to accept his loss, thinking something like: "Oh well. We have to let go of everything sooner or later. No point suffering over what you can't change. I have had such wonderful times traveling around this vast land with that Harley. Now I hope that it gives such pleasure to its new owner."

He was so pleased that the thief had only stolen his motorbike and not his peace of mind. He had successfully passed a hard test in letting go.

As he was walking away to catch public transport, smiling to himself at his spiritual achievement, he suddenly realized that he was on the wrong floor of the garage!

When he went down the stairs to the correct level, there was his Harley, smiling at him as it were. Not only had he passed the letting go test, he still had his motorbike. He had won twice over.

Well done, Patrick.

60. On the Ledge

A famous painter had a bad accident on his Harley Davidson. When he woke up in hospital, the surgeon told him the bad news that they had to amputate his hand, the one he used to paint with. The painter was devastated. He had lost the ability to do the one thing he loved most in the world. With it, he had lost his life's purpose.

As soon as he was discharged from the hospital, he entered a tall office block in the city, took the elevator to an upper floor, found an empty office, and climbed out on to the ledge. He was going to kill himself.

As he gazed the long distance down to the ground, he saw an amazing sight. There on the sidewalk was a man with no arms at all, dancing with joy along the street!

"My God!" he thought to himself, "I've only lost one hand, and there's a guy with no hands at all, not even arms, and he's dancing! What do I want to kill myself for?"

He decided to live. He stepped back from the ledge and into the empty office.

He thought to himself, "I have to find out that man's secret—how can he be so happy with no hands?"

He ran to the elevator, quickly reaching the ground floor, and running along the street he found the man. An armless man isn't hard to find.

"Thank you! Thank you, sir! You've just saved my life. I'm an artist and have lost my painting hand in a motorcycle accident. I was so depressed that I climbed up to the top of that building over there and was about to commit suicide. While standing on the edge, I looked down and saw you, with no arms at all, dancing along the street! Please tell me, how are you still so happy after losing both your arms?"

The armless man paused for a moment.

"Actually I wasn't dancing. I was just trying to scratch my bum."

How else does an armless man deal with an itchy bottom?

61. My Mother's Shelf

A couple of years after moving to Australia, I went to visit my mother in London. One of my supporters kindly donated a soft toy kangaroo to give to my mum as a present from Australia.

My mother loved that gift. She placed it proudly on the shelf in her living room, where she spent most of the time. It would remind her of me after I'd returned to Australia. I was happy too. I'd found a gift that my mother would cherish.

A few years later, when I visited London again, I bought my mother a soft toy koala bear, to go with the toy kangaroo. She loved that, too, and placed it on her shelf next to the kangaroo.

The next time I visited, I gave her a soft toy kookaburra, and the time after, a toy platypus. Her shelf was getting crowded with memorabilia from Australia.

On my fifth visit, I presented her with a big, soft and cuddly toy wombat. She loved that too. But when she tried to put it on her shelf, together with the kangaroo, koala, kookaburra, and platypus, there wasn't enough space. Things would fall off. Then my mother would try and squeeze them in, and more stuff would fall off.

"Why don't you give some of the old stuffed animals away, Mum?" I suggested. "Then there'll be some space for the new animals."

"Nooooo!" she moaned. "They are all too precious." She spent hours trying to fit everything on her shelf.

This is called stress. Sometimes you just can't fit everything into your brain. You try to put one more thing in, and other things fall out, like the animals on my mother's shelf. Soon the shelf is so overburdened it breaks. For the brain, that's called a mental breakdown. Once you understand what's going on, then such suffering is easy to avoid.

Had my mother given the old soft toy away, to a friend or to a charity, then not only would there be enough space on her shelf for the new presents, but they would have had less competition for her attention and so been enjoyed all the more.

Make your mind like an empty shelf, with enough space for enjoying the gift that is always new, the present.

62. Fifty strokes of the cat

Ours is a strict monastery. It takes two years of disciplined training before one can become a monk. I call it "quality control." Even in the first year of training, the wannabe monk has to keep the precept of eating no solid food from noon until the dawn of the next day.

One morning, one such postulant came to see me. He was English and in his mid twenties. He told me that he felt very, very guilty about something he had done the day before. He had not been able to sleep the previous night. He had come to me for a confession.

From beneath a drooping head, too ashamed to keep eye contact, he admitted that, late the previous afternoon, he was so hungry that he'd snuck into the monastery kitchen, made himself a sandwich, and eaten it. He had broken one of his training precepts.

"Very good," I told him.

He glanced up.

"It is very good that you're being honest and telling me what you've done. Now try to eat more at our 11:00 lunchtime, and if you are still hungry, you can drink some fruit juice or have a honey drink, which are allowable. You may even eat some dark chocolate, that's okay too. Now you may go."

"What? Aren't you going to punish me?"

"No, we don't do punishments in Buddhist monasteries."

"That's not good enough," he continued. "I know my character. If you don't give me penance, I'll just do the same thing again."

I was on the spot. How does one deal with such a person who believes that only punishment can train one to be disciplined? Then an idea came to me.

The previous day, I had been reading Robert Hughes' historical novel about early Australia called *The Fatal Shore*. The book describes the extremely brutal punishments inflicted on convicts using a vicious whip called the "cat o' nine tails," or "the cat" for short.

"Okay," I told our miscreant postulant, "I'll give you a punishment, a traditional Australian punisment. I will give you . . . fifty strokes of the cat!"

The poor boy's face drained of color. His lips started to quiver (so much for the English stiff upper lip). He was thinking "Oh no! The abbot is going to flog me. That's not what I meant by a penance."

Because he was new to Buddhism, he actually believed he was going to be whipped for stealing a sandwich. Then I explained to him what "fifty strokes of the cat" meant in a Buddhist monastery.

We had two cats at the time. "Please find one of those cats and stroke it fifty times," I told him. "Learn some compassion from stroking the cat, and then you might learn how to forgive yourself. That is the secret of discipline."

He took his punishment very well.

So did our cat.

63. The General with the Best Discipline in the Army

In the Chinese classic *The Art of War,* there is a story about the general with the best-disciplined soldiers in the imperial army. He was summoned by the emperor to explain how it is that his soldiers always followed his orders.

"They always follow my orders, Sire," he explained, "because I only tell them to do what they already want to do."

Why did the soldiers want to get up so early in the morning? Why did they look forward to grueling training sessions? And how was it that they were eager to go into battle, where they might get wounded or even killed?

The answer is that the general was such a compelling motivator that his soldiers were already convinced before he even gave the orders.

They wanted to get up early and train hard. They had been motivated by inspiring talks on heroism and patriotism to want to go to battle for the cause. That was the secret of their perfect discipline— they had a charismatic leader who motivated them.

Punishment rarely leads to discipline. Instead, it teaches people to be smart enough not to get caught. But when you can motivate your son to come home early from a night out so his studies do not suffer, instead of punishing him, then you get discipline.

64. Girlfriend power

The son of one of my friends was staying out late with his girlfriend many nights a week, and his university grades were suffering as a result. Like most boys his age, he would not listen to his parents. So his father, a very smart man, found another way to help his son be more disciplined.

In the early hours one morning, when his son arrived home with his girlfriend after a night of clubbing, his father was standing outside waiting for them.

"Come inside," he motioned.

His son thought that he was in *big* trouble, but his dad never even spoke to him. Instead he addressed his son's girlfriend. "You've being dating my son for quite a long time now, haven't you?"

"Yes, she replied.

"I don't know what your plans are, but who knows, you two may decide to get married some day. Now, I'm sure you wouldn't want a husband who failed his degree and can't get a good job. If my son keeps staying out so late, that may very well happen. Has he mentioned that his grades have been falling close to failing since he began going out with you?"

"No," she replied, looking sharply at her boyfriend, "I didn't know."

"Just thought I should tell you," said the father. "Goodnight." And he left them alone.

From that night on, the young man's girlfriend made sure that they always returned home early, and she kept a close watch over his grades, which improved dramatically. He eventually completed his degree, and he now has a good job.

So if you have an undisciplined son who won't listen to his parents, try girlfriend power. If you get her on board, you have leverage. Or try enlisting your daughter's boyfriend to help keep her on the right path.

65. Twenty Push-ups Every Morning

People are really into fitness these days. They spend a lot of their spare time at the gym, or playing sports, to maintain a healthy body. Yet they still have unhealthy emotions. They get angry and depressed too easily.

Therefore, I have developed and taught a simple exercise regime to develop healthy emotions. It is called "twenty push-ups every morning."

After going to the toilet in the morning and brushing your teeth, stand with your feet about fifteen inches apart on a warm, soft mat in front of a mirror. Breathe in and out deeply for three or four breaths to relax yourself. Then raise your hands to the level of your face. Place your index fingers on the corners of your mouth. Then looking in the mirror, push up.

One!

Let your mouth return to its usual miserable-looking position for three seconds, then push up again.

Two!

Continue for twenty repetitions. Don't cut the number short!

Not only will you laugh at yourself every morning, but the muscles around the corners of your mouth will be exercised so effectively that it will be easy to laugh at life and smile much longer than ever.

All it takes is a bit of training.

66. Tummy Wisdom

When I was a boy, being of ample girth was considered a sign of health and carefree happiness. The spiritual exemplar who inspired me in those days with his kindness and social conscience was Friar Tuck from the TV series *Robin Hood*. He was fat as well as wise and jolly. That was the sort of monk I aspired to emulate.

Nowadays we're all supposed to be thin and serious. I started to succumb to concern about the size of my ample tummy when, one evening in my temple in Perth, a Chinese woman came up to me and began rubbing my tummy for good luck! So I did some urgent research.

I found that experiments have shown that when you are happy, especially when you laugh, the blood vessels in your body expand significantly. But when you are miserable and worried, they become much thinner.

This explained so much.

Perhaps you've noticed, as I have, that most older people who are fat are jolly and kind, like Santa Claus. I reasoned that this must be because they laugh so easily and often that their blood vessels have expanded as wide as super-highways, and all the bad cholesterol and other "guck" easily finds a way through. Since miserable fat people have narrow blood vessels, which are easily clogged, they must die sooner, leaving only the happy ones behind.

So for those of you who are overweight, like this author, make sure you laugh a lot. The effect on your arteries may save your life!

For example, the famous American comedian George Burns, during an interview on his ninety-something birthday, was asked about his lifestyle: "George, you're in your late nineties, and still you stay out into the early hours of the morning in nightclubs, drink copious amounts of scotch whiskey, smoke cigars by the box, and eat fatty foods. Aren't you concerned about your health?"

"Not at all," replied George. "My wife was always worried about my health and lifestyle, and that's why she died many years ago!"

67. The origin of stress

In 2010, I was invited to give a keynote address at the World Computer Congress in Brisbane. I knew nothing about computers, but such trivial details as "not knowing what I am talking about" didn't stop me from accepting the gig.

During my speech, I held up my glass of water and asked my audience, "How heavy is this glass?"

Before they could answer, I continued, "If I keep on holding my glass like this, after five minutes my arm will ache. After ten minutes, I will be in considerable pain. And after fifteen minutes, I will be in agony and a very stupid monk!

"So what should I do?

"Whenever the glass of water starts to feel too heavy for me to hold comfortably, I should put it down for one minute. Having rested my arm for sixty seconds, then I can pick up the glass and carry it again with ease. If you don't believe me, try it yourself at home!

"This is the origin of stress at your workplace. It has nothing to do with how much work you have to do, nor how heavy your responsibilities are. It has everything to do with not knowing how to put the work down when it feels too heavy to bear, and rest for a little while, before picking up the burden again."

My advice was so well received that it was published in *The Australian*, the only national daily newspaper in Australia, and migrated from there to the Australian Stock Exchange website.

If you don't learn to "put down the burden" and take a rest when you feel stressed, then the quality of your work will decline, your output will get much less, and your stress levels will increase. But if you give yourself a half-hour break in the middle of the day, the thirty minutes that you lose is soon made up with higher-quality work completed in less time. You get, for example, four hours work done in three hours, and it is of good quality. Putting down the glass of water, therefore, is not a waste of precious time but an investment, repaid later through the increased efficiency of your brain.

My advice later appeared on the Harvard Business School blog. So maybe I do know what I am talking about after all!

68. Half a Sheet of Paper

Many years ago, I read the following inspiring story of how a man overcame his anger and lack of self-esteem.

A widow was presenting the eulogy at her husband's funeral service. She held up a dog-eared half sheet of paper, explained that her husband had kept it in his wallet since before they were married, and that it had prevented him from getting angry with others or becoming negative about himself.

Her husband had told her that when he was a teenager attending an all-boys high school, a major fight was about to break out in his classroom. It had been brewing for days. The teacher used the last opportunity to exert her authority to order every student to stay at his desk and carefully tear out a page from his exercise book. Then she told them to write, at the top of the page, the name of the boy in the class that they hated the most. They all obeyed. Then she ordered them to draw a neat vertical line down the middle of the page and, on the left side of that line, write the reasons why they hate that boy so much. Her class happily followed that instruction too.

"Now," she commanded, "on the right side of the line, write the things that you admire and respect about that boy you hate."

That was very hard for the boys to do. She had to force them to complete the task.

"Fold your piece of paper carefully along the vertical line," was her next instruction, "and tear it in half. I am coming around with a wastebasket. The left-hand pieces of paper, where you have written all the reasons why you hate your enemy, I want you to place in the wastebasket. The right-hand pieces of paper, where you have written the things that you respect and admire about your enemy, you must politely hand to them. *Do it!*"

The widow explained that the old half sheet of paper that she was holding up was the right-hand piece that her husband's worst enemy at high school had given to him, describing all the things that he respected and admired in her husband when he was a boy.

Her husband would refer to that half sheet of paper whenever he was about to get angry. If this is what his worst enemy could see in him, maybe he could bring himself to see some redeeming qualities in his own enemies. Then when he was close to becoming depressed, he thought that if his enemy could see such fine characteristics to admire in him, then maybe he could see them too. That is why he kept the half sheet of paper with him all his life. It made him a contented man.

So if you don't like yourself, get out a sheet of paper, draw a line down the center, write the things that you don't like about yourself on the left side and the things you like about yourself on the right side. You must fill the right side! Then tear it in half, throw away the left side, and keep the right portion. Refer to it regularly. It will provide you self-esteem—and also save you spending a lot of money on therapy!

69. Dealing with BIG Trouble

While teaching in Malaysia, my hosts asked if I would see a friend of theirs who was in *big* trouble. She had been to psychologists and therapists, but no one had been able to help her. They thought perhaps I could help.

I did not know what her problem was, but I did know that if all the best professionals had not been able to help her, then I would have to do something very different. Indeed it is not hard for a monk to think "outside the box," because we actually live outside the box.

When she came in to see me, I made my mind empty of all thoughts. Being a professional meditator, it is something very easy for me to do. Then she proceeded to tell me how she had been brutally raped.

After she had finished the harrowing story, I heard these words come out from a place within my empty mind and through my mouth: "You are so fortunate to have been raped!"

I was shocked at what I had said. The woman in front of me was even more stunned. These words had not been premeditated. They just came out from a very quiet place in my mind by themselves. I soon made sense of them. I told her:

"I will never be able to comprehend what you have gone through and how you must feel. But what I have seen is that you have substantial inner spiritual strength. You will find your way out of this horrible hole, and when you do, you will be able to say something that I'm incapable of saying. You'll be able to look deeply into the eyes of another victim of rape and tell her 'I understand how you feel, for I've been there too.' Then you'll be able to do even more. You will be able to tell her the way out, saying, 'Take my hand. I know how to get out of this horrible hole.' I'll never be able to do that. That is what I meant when I said 'You are so fortunate to have been raped.' You will later help so many others."

The woman understood. Somehow, my words had given the terrible experience a meaning and given her an important task to perform, not just for herself, but also for the comfort of many others.

70. Kissing the Ugly Frog

Once upon a winter time, a poor young maiden in rags was collecting firewood in the snow-covered forest to heat her drafty little hut. There among the fallen wood, she saw the ugliest frog that had ever existed. "Urghh!" she shrieked. "I think I'm gonna throw up!"

Then the grotesque frog spoke: "Please don't throw up yet. Help me instead. I'm really an unfortunate boy. I had a spell put on me by a wicked witch who didn't like my music. Kiss me and the spell will be broken. In return I will make you wealthy and be your servant."

So the poor girl closed her eyes and kissed the frog.

The frog didn't turn into a prince, because these days royalty have too many bodyguards for wicked witches to come close enough to cast any spell. No, it was much better than that. The frog changed into a famous pop singer, cuter than Justin Bieber and just as rich. They started a relationship and now live happily ever after in a mansion in Malibu.

Such is the oldest fairy story, with a little twist. But what is its meaning?

There are many "ugly frogs" in our modern life. Your mother-in-law may be one of them (If you rearrange the letters in "mother-in-law" it spells "Hitler-woman"!). So how can you "kiss" such an ugly frog as the stereotypical mother-in-law?

A young Buddhist wife could not get along with her husband's mum, even though she tried. No matter what the daughter-in-law said or did, it was never, ever good enough. The mother-in-law would always find fault with her. It was driving the young wife crazy.

The daughter-in-law tried meditating. That didn't work.

Then she tried spreading loving-kindness to her mother-in-law every morning and evening. That didn't work either.

Next she tried Buddhist chanting, but to no avail. The mother-in-law was just as critical of her as ever.

Being a Mahayana Buddhist, the young wife would often pray to the goddess of mercy, Kuan Yin. So early one morning she tried praying.

She must have been exhausted from all the worry about her mother-in-law because she fell asleep while praying and dreamed of Kuan Yin. There was the goddess of mercy in her flowing white robe holding the vessel of kindness, but when she looked at Kuan Yin's face, she was shocked. The face was not the usual one that is seen on all statues of Kuan Yin in the temple. Instead, Kuan Yin had her mother-in-law's face!

It was a sign. From that time on, the young wife regarded her difficult mother-in-law as an embodiment of the goddess of mercy.

With such a fundamental change in her attitude toward her mother-in-law, she received less negativity. The mother-in-law began to like her daughter-in-law, and they soon became the best of friends.

How you regard others will be how others regard you. That is how to kiss an ugly frog and remove the wicked spell.

71. How Not to Pray

Some years ago, there were very bad floods in Queensland, Australia. A Buddhist monk was stranded on the roof of his temple, and the waters were rising, when a rescue boat came to save him.

"Jump in the boat, Venerable Sir," said the boat's captain respectfully. "We've come to rescue you."

"No need," replied the monk, matter of factly. "I'm a follower of Kuan Yin, the goddess of mercy. I have faith Kuan Yin will save me. Please, carry on."

"The flood will get worse," said the captain. "You can pray to your god in the boat."

"Don't mock me!" protested the monk. "Kuan Yin will save me. You'll see!"

The monk resisted all persuasion to get into the boat until it could wait no longer. The boat left to help others.

Soon, the floodwaters rose, and the monk was clinging on to the curly ornaments on the ends of the temple roof's ridge, which every Buddhist temple must have, when a second boat came.

"Venerable Sir," they shouted, "you're a legend! We're all very impressed with the strength of your belief, really, we are! Now jump in the boat! The water is rising fast."

"No way!" replied the monk. "This is a test of faith. I've prayed to Kuan Yin all my long life. She won't let me down now. Kuan Yin will save me. Leave me and save the others. "

"What if you're wrong?" asked the captain.

"I'm not wrong!" exclaimed the monk. "You'll see!"

No matter what the rescue crew said, that monk would not jump into the boat. So they left.

The floodwaters rose some more, and the monk was holding on to the temple's TV aerial when a helicopter came and lowered a ladder.

"Monk!" they shouted down from a megaphone. "Listen up! You've proven your faith, okay? Now grab on to the damn ladder. We're pulling you up."

"Kuan Yin will save me!!" screamed the monk.

"Grab hold. *Now!*"

"I have faith!"

And still he refused. The helicopter had no choice but to move on, leaving the monk behind.

You know what happened next?

The waters rose and the monk drowned.

When that monk appeared in heaven, he was very, very angry. He went looking for the goddess of mercy, and when he found her, he blasted her. "I had such faith in you, and you let me down! I told all those nonbelievers that you would save me, and you didn't. I'm so humiliated and so . . . so . . . so dead! Why didn't you save me?"

Kuan Yin smiled and softly replied, "Didn't I send two boats and a helicopter?"

Now you understand how not to pray!

72. The Blind Leading the Blind

A famous monastery in the mountains of northern India, well known for its highly attained monks, had recently elected a new abbot who was also their spiritual leader. As it was getting close to winter, the young monks asked their new teacher whether it was going to be a cold season or a mild one.

The new abbot's meditation was not yet developed enough to predict the weather. However, to be on the safe side and impress his disciples, he said that it was going to be a cold winter and that the monks should collect a lot of firewood.

A few days later, he had the idea to call the local weather station and ask the professor of meteorology, who happened to have the highest qualifications from Oxford University. "Professor," asked the anonymous caller, "what type of winter can we expect this year?"

"Signs indicate it will be a cold winter," said the professor.

Thus it was that, the following day, the abbot told his monks to collect even more firewood.

A week later, the abbot made another anonymous call to the weather station, "Does it still look like a cold winter, professor?"

"The signs are looking worse, sir," replied the professor. "It looks like it will be a very cold winter."

The next morning the abbot announced to his monks that they should collect every piece of wood that they could find because he foresaw that it was going to be one of the coldest winters ever seen in the mountains.

Thinking he might have gone too far, and that if he was wrong his reputation would be lost, the abbot called the head of the local weather station again. "Professor, are you absolutely certain that the signs are predicting a very cold winter?"

"Absolutely!" replied the professor. "In fact the signs are getting worse by the day. This looks like it will be an extremely cold winter indeed."

"How can you be so sure?" asked the anonymous caller.

"Because," answered the learned professor, "all the holy monks in our local monastery are collecting firewood like mad."

The friend who sent me this story said that it is a metaphor for how the stock market works. He may be right!

73. The Bad Elephant

A local zoo had a gentle elephant called Ellie. All the children who visited the zoo loved playing with Ellie. She didn't mind them stroking her long trunk or giving them rides through the zoo grounds. In fact she liked the attention. Sometimes, when the children had gone home and it was quiet at night, Ellie would gaze up at the stars and reminisce about the thick forests where she grew up and roamed wherever she wanted. She also remembered the times she was almost killed by hunters as well as the days when she went hungry because no food could be found. It was a comfortable life in the zoo, with delicious and plentiful food, free medical care, and an air-conditioned enclosure where she could escape the heat of the day. She was a happy elephant.

Then something changed. One day, some school children visiting the zoo were teasing Ellie about the size of her ears. Ellie squirted water from her trunk all over them, soaking them all, including their teacher. Later, while her keeper was cleaning the elephant excrement out from her cage, Ellie pushed the keeper over headfirst into the pile of poo, which was large. Ellie was becoming bad. Soon, she was throwing rotten fruit at her visitors and refused to let children anywhere near her.

The zookeepers called in the vet to see if some sickness had made Ellie bad. But the elephant doctor found no such sign of sickness. Then they tried an elephant psychologist, who suggested menopause just because Ellie was a female, but the doctor soon ruled that out. Meanwhile Ellie was becoming more ill-tempered by the day.

Then someone suggested that it might be a spiritual crisis, a sort of elephantine dark night of the soul.

So they called in a monk.

The venerable monk could only come late in the evening after his duties were completed. So late one night, when the zoo was closed to visitors, the monk meditated alone in the dark just outside Ellie's enclosure.

Around eleven, the monk's meditation was disturbed by the sound of low menacing whispers and demonic laughter. Was it a ghost? Were these the sound of vampires? They were coming from right behind Ellie's enclosure.

The monk rose from his meditation and went to find out. The monk saw that there was a gardening shop next to the zoo, and in the rear of the shop's yard, right behind where Ellie was sleeping, some shifty men and women were having a secret meeting. Creeping closer, the monk could hear that they were drug dealers, discussing their evening's nefarious business. A jar for flowers was not the only pot that was being sold in that shop. The dealers were also discussing the vicious punishments to be given to those who could not pay their drug debts. The cause of Ellie's change in character now became clear.

The following evening, the police were waiting for those drug dealers and arrested them all. In their place, the monk arranged some of his friends to meditate and talk of all the kind and generous things that they had done or planned to do, and how they would forgive those who had let them down. They also softly chanted the verses on spreading love throughout the whole world, to all beings, especially to elephants.

Ellie started to become kinder and more gentle. After a few days, she was back to her old lovable self, happily playing with even the naughtiest of children.

That story is adapted from an old tale taught by the Buddha. It shows how even animals are influenced by the behavior of others. So if you have a partner who is becoming more ill-tempered by the day, or a teenage son or daughter who is driving you crazy, lock them up in a monastery for a few days. They may become soft or kind like the monks—that is, unless the monks become ill-tempered like them!

74. Hearing voices

A friend of mine was relaxing at home on his sofa, reading *Who Ordered This Truckload of Dung?*, when suddenly he heard a strange sound, almost like a whisper. He paused reading, and leaning forward, listened carefully.

". . . hey," it seemed to say.

He glanced around the room, but no one was there.

"Hey." he heard again, this time louder.

The door was closed and the windows shut, so he decided he must be imagining things. With a shrug of the shoulders, he nestled back into the sofa and went back to reading.

"HEY!" came a shout this time, and he jumped back, nearly toppling over the sofa. This time, it was so strong and so clear, he couldn't be imagining things.

"Go to the casino," the voice said.

Now, it's not every day that you receive supernatural help for your finances. Trusting in the voices from beyond, he decided to go gambling. He got dressed, took some cash, and before he knew it was stepping through the revolving glass doors into the world of flashing lights and raucous punters.

As he walked in, the voice spoke again, "Go to the roulette table. Place a hundred dollars on number 6." Following the voice, he made his way to a crowded table and placed the bet.

The croupier spun the wheel and slung in the ball. The ball landed on number 6.

"Yeah!" he heard the divine voice say.

There was a murmur in the crowd. He had just won a considerable amount of money. My friend was excited.

"Place all the winnings on number 17! Place all the winnings on number 17!" he heard the voice say. Buzzing from the win, he did just so.

With a raised eyebrow, the croupier spun the wheel once more. The crowd held its breath in anticipation. This would be a big win. And guess what? It hit number 17.

"Woo hoo!" the voice cheered along with the crowd, exploding in excitement. People began elbowing in to watch the mystery unfold, the table now awash with bodies.

My friend was up to $100,000!

He clutched the table, breathing rapidly. The room around him was spinning, a kaleidoscope of flashing lights. He made out the gaze of the croupier, who gave him a broad smile. He sensed this man was on his side.

"Do you wish to continue?" the croupier asked gently.

"Put the whole lot on number 23! Put the whole lot on number 23!" urged the divine voice again, and that seemed to be the answer.

He took pause. Winning this throw would be astronomical. He'd never have to work again. He'd be set for life. Amid the mayhem, he searched in his heart for the answer. The crowd looked on.

After a few moments, he took a deep breath and went all in.

"That's it! Go for it, son!" yelled one of the punters, breaking the silence, and with whistles and claps the crowd urged on.

The croupier, now wide-eyed, swung the ball in . . . and round and round it twirled, as if forever. Our friend could hardly breathe. The crowd now demanded silence, and a hush fell. No one spoke a word.

The wheel spun and spun, and then began slowing to a stop . . . It landed in number 23!

A few members of the crowd shouted out in amazement, but others stood frozen, holding on to each other in tension, for they could see what our friend saw.

The ball was bouncing around in slot 23, teetering on the edge as the wheel spun round. The ball was poised on the edge, the wheel spinning in slow motion. It finally tumbled, and before our friend could shout for joy, it bounced out, and into number 24.

The crowd was stunned. Our friend had lost everything.

In the deathly silence, he heard the supernatural voice once more, "Oh shit! Sorry! Oh shit!"

Even supernatural voices make mistakes, so don't trust them. Believe in your common sense instead.

People gamble because they stupidly think that by listening to divine voices, by praying at churches or temples, or by making promises such as "I will give up smoking if you will let me win," then they can beat the system. You are no different than anyone else. You cannot beat the system. The system will beat you!

It is just the same as a soccer fan watching an important match on TV at home who shouts out "Pass the ball! Shoot! Come on!" They actually think that they can influence the game by all their screaming and hollering. Consider this rationally, you are shouting at a television set. The players are hundreds of miles away and cannot hear you! You are impotent, so sit down, watch the game, and shut up.

It is just like the gambler who shouts at the slot machine, "Come on! Come on!" Slot machines do not have ears. They cannot hear your prayers. You have no power to beat the odds. When you let go of your conceit that you are different from everybody else, when you understand that no one can beat the odds, then you will give up gambling.

75. Monks and Nuns Beating the Odds

I don't know why it is, but Buddhist monks and nuns seem to be able to beat the odds, which may be why we are not permitted to gamble.

A well-known Buddhist nun had just finished teaching a meditation retreat in the UK and had stopped for lunch on her way to Heathrow airport. The restaurant that they chose was attached to an English pub, and they had to pass through the bar to enter the dining room. After their lunch, the driver decided to get rid of a small number of English coins in the jackpot (pokie) machine in the bar. She had just inserted a two-pound coin when the Buddhist nun walked past.

"You have all the good karma, Sister. You pull the handle," said the driver.

In a moment's lapse of mindfulness, the Buddhist nun pulled that handle. The wheels went round before stopping one by one.

Jackpot! The bells rang and lights flashed as thousands of pounds poured out of the machine onto the nun's simple patchwork robe.

Patrons in the pub fell silent and stared. The barman picked up a small bell and began ringing it. Then he announced to the stunned nun that, according to long-standing tradition, whoever wins the jackpot must buy a round of drinks for everyone in the bar!

Thus it was that for the first time in 2,500 years since the Buddha meditated on this earth, a Buddhist nun bought whiskeys, gin and tonics, and beer for dozens of happy customers in a bar.

As for my own gambling story, a few years ago a disciple asked me to bless his friend's new shop. My mistake was not asking what type of shop it was.

When I arrived in the shopping mall early one morning for the ceremony, I discovered that it was a stall selling only one product, lottery tickets! It was too late for me to get out of performing the ceremony, so I blessed the lotto stall with as much gusto as I would bless a doctor's clinic.

A couple of years later, I was reading the weekend newspaper when I saw a feature article on that same lottery stall that was entitled "The Luckiest Lottery Shop in Australia." And where is that shop? I am not telling. Also, I am not blessing any more lottery shops!

76. The Miracle

As someone trained in theoretical physics at Cambridge University, I'm not that open to the occurrence of miracles. But there was one event I witnessed that has no other explanation.

It was the thirtieth anniversary of our Buddhist Society of Western Australia. We had come such a long way from the most humble of beginnings, and it was time to celebrate our success and show that Buddhism had arrived in Western Australia. We hired the most central open-air location in Perth, the Supreme Court Gardens, which to our amazement was free that day. We ordered a huge new golden Buddha statue from Thailand for the occasion. No expense was spared for the stage, tents, food, and entertainment. We managed to persuade the premier of Western Australia, the Honorable Dr. Geoff Gallop, to attend, as well as ambassadors and other dignitaries. The event was to occur on a Sunday evening on the full moon of May, which is the holiest night in the Buddhist calendar. It was such immense hard work, but gradually everything was coming together.

On the morning of the event, I woke up to heavy rain. The forecast said it was to get much worse. A storm warning had been issued for Perth, with the main part of the storm expected to hit Perth at 7:00 p.m., precisely when the ceremony was to begin.

As we set things up throughout the day, we all got soaked to the skin in continual heavy rain. Three times, the premier's office called me to ask, "Are you cancelling? The storm is forecast to get worse!"

Three times I replied, "No way!" A good friend, who had spent his whole working life as a merchant seaman, pointed at the falling barometric pressure and explained that a lifetime of experience at sea told him that a bad storm was certainly coming. Even one of my monks took me aside and advised me to stop making a fool of myself and cancel. I refused again.

Fifteen minutes before the first VIP arrived, a worker came into the tent where I was making some final adjustments, sobbing, "Come out! Come out!" My thought was that something had gone terribly wrong, but all she did was point upward to the sky. The clouds had parted for the first time that day to reveal the splendid full moon.

The rain had stopped.

Soon the premier arrived with all the other dignitaries. A film crew was following me repeating again and again, "This is weird! This is weird!" We conducted the ceremony in dry weather under the radiant full moon.

Once the ceremony was completed, the clouds closed in and the rain poured down all night. The following morning, the event site was under two inches of water, and the nearby freeway was also flooded. Many people who were invited never came, because in the surrounding suburbs the rain lashed down without stopping and many trees were uprooted. They couldn't believe that we held the ceremony in dry conditions. The company that hired out the stage and tents wrote an email saying, "We don't know who this Ajahn Brahm is, but we would like to ask him who is going to win at the racetrack today."

This was not a mere shower that had cleared but a massive storm, and only over the site for our ceremony.

There is no other explanation—it was a miracle.

77. Divine Intervention

A young American had just finished his work for the Peace Corps in Thailand when he decided to extend his stay and try out the lifestyle of a Buddhist monk. He was staying in a hotel in Bangkok and, not knowing where to go to become a monk, asked the hotel concierge for advice. It was not the usual request made of the concierge in a Bangkok hotel, so it was not surprising that the advice he was given was not that accurate.

The young American was told to go to a monastery called Wat Bovornives in central Bangkok, where some Western monks sometimes reside. He was advised to take along some food to offer to the monks on their early-morning almsround and then to ask one of those monks for ordination.

He followed the advice and arrived outside the locked monastery around 4:00 in the morning. As he walked up and down the deserted street wondering what to do, an elderly Thai gentleman approached him and asked in perfect English if he could be of any help. When the American explained his purpose, the Thai man answered that the monastery gates would not open until 5:30 but, as he had the key, he would show him around until the monks came out.

The Thai gentleman opened an iron gate that led to the main ordination hall, turned on the lights, opened the beautiful carved doors, and led the young man inside. For the next hour, the Thai gentleman gave a detailed and fascinating description of the traditional

Thai paintings on the building's walls, including who sponsored the works and why. Some were donated to make merit for a deceased parent or to restore to health a sickly child. The hour flew by and, after completing the description of the final mural, the Thai man told the American to go wait outside, as a senior Thai monk would be coming out soon. He was to put the food in the monk's bowl and then ask for ordination. Meanwhile, the Thai gentleman would lock up.

The American did as he was advised and was later led into the monastery by the senior monk to begin the basic training before he would be given ordination as a Buddhist monk.

However, there was a problem. The American could not understand the English of the Thai monk assigned to train him. "Can I have another monk to teach me?" he asked.

"This is the best English speaker in the whole monastery," he was told.

"What about that elderly Thai man who met me on that first day? The one who opened the iron gate and led me inside the ordination hall. He spoke perfect English," replied the American.

The monks immediately took the young man to the elderly abbot in his office. As he told the story, the abbot stopped him and called in his secretary to write this all down.

You see, there was no layman who had the key to that gate. Indeed, that gate is called the Royal Gate, and only the kings and princes of Thailand are allowed to use that entrance. This was the monastery where the kings of Thailand are ordained for temporary periods. The lights cannot be switched on at the place the American described. No layman has the keys to the most sacred building in the whole monastery. And not even the old abbot knew so much about the temple's murals.

Then the abbot asked the American to describe this elderly Thai gentleman. All the American could say, at first, was that he was wearing traditional Thai dress, not normally seen these days. Then, when pressed for more detail, the young American looked up and stared in amazement. On the wall of the abbot's office was a portrait of that elderly Thai gentleman.

"It was him!" exclaimed the American. "That's the man who met me."

That was a portrait of His Majesty King Rama the Fifth, otherwise known as King Chulalongkorn. He died on October 23, 1910. Now his entry through the Royal Gate made sense, and he knew all the details of the murals because his family members were the main sponsors. A former Thai king, now certainly a heavenly being, had helped a young man pursue his goal of becoming a Buddhist monk.

78. The Know-It-All

The former kings of Thailand used to surround themselves with the cleverest people in the land. One such courtier was as sharp as a razor and just as cutting. His fellow courtiers planned to seek his comeuppance by embarrassing him in front of His Majesty.

Their plan was to praise his many abilities before the king, puffing up his ego so much that he would rashly admit to having the ability to read the minds of others. Then they would challenge him to reveal what they were thinking. Even if that smart aleck guessed what they were actually thinking, they would firmly say that he was wrong. Because who can prove what someone is thinking?

Thus, one morning at court, minister after minister praised the great wisdom and abilities of this courtier in the presence of the king. When they thought that his pride had got the better of his prudence, one minister exclaimed, "This man is so gifted, he can probably read the thoughts of others. Is that true?"

"Of course I can," said the courtier with pride.

The others smiled at each other. He had fallen into their crafty trap.

"Okay. So please tell His Majesty what we are all thinking now."

They had caught him. There was no escape for that know-it-all.

"Your Majesty," replied the courtier, "I will tell you what all your ministers are thinking right now. They are all thinking kind and devoted thoughts toward their king."

The ministers considered for a few seconds and agreed, "Yes, Your Majesty, we are all thinking such thoughts!"

That is omniscience.

79. A Tale of Two Mango Trees

The Buddha told the story of a powerful king who was returning to the palace after supervising a training exercise for his army. He passed two mango trees, one of which was dripping with fragrant, ripe mangoes, while the other bore no fruit at all. He spurned the tree without fruit while resolving to return later to the fertile tree, after having changed out of his military uniform, to enjoy a mango feast.

When the king returned, he found that the tree with so many ripe mangoes had been violently stripped of all its fruit. His soldiers had not waited to get changed before gorging themselves. Worse, that tree now had so many broken branches and fallen leaves that it appeared deformed and sickly. The mango tree that had no fruit, on the other hand, was untouched by the army and looked healthy and strong.

The wise king abdicated the next day and went forth as a monk. Being a wealthy king was like being that tree with much fruit. Scheming ministers and princes, and even neighboring nations, coveted his wealth. It was only a matter of time before they would attack and he would be injured or killed, just like that once fruitful tree had been badly disfigured. Better having few possessions, like a monk; then he could live like that tree without mangoes—healthy, strong, and always ready to give cool shade to others.

80. How to Catch a Mango

In my first few months at Wat Pah Pong monastery with my teacher, Ajahn Chah, he would repeat the following story again and again. It was such nonsense that I dismissed it as some cultural anomaly. Yet somehow I remembered it. Later in my life as a monk, I recognized the metaphor as the perfect description of how enlightenment happens, offered by the most brilliant master I ever met.

Wat Pah Pong is a mango orchard, whose trees were planted by the Buddha. The trees are now mature, with thousands of ripe mangoes ready to be eaten. Because of the great wisdom and compassion of the Buddha, monks and nuns today, and lay followers too, don't need to climb the tree to get a mango. Nor do they need to throw sticks up, or shake the tree, to get a mango to fall.

All one needs to do is to sit perfectly still under the mango tree, open a hand, and a mango will fall into it.

Such is the wisdom and compassion of the Buddha.

I knew mango trees. If you just sat underneath a mango tree, you would have to wait many days for a mango to fall. The birds would probably eat them all first. Moreover, if one did actually fall, it would more likely drop on my bald head, knowing my luck, than into my hand. This was a stupid simile!

Now I realize that it was I who was stupid. Nothing is gained in the spiritual life when you go "shaking the tree" or "throwing up sticks" or "climbing the tree" to make things happen. When you learn to be perfectly still, without a desire in the world, and open up your heart with unconditional love, only then do the mangoes of enlightenment fall softly into your hand.

81. Forbidden Fruit

A poor farmer had a lot of moldy hay. Instead of wasting it, he tried to feed it to his cows, but the cows would rather go hungry than eat the bad-tasting grass.

So the farmer mixed the moldy hay with some fresh hay and gave it to his cows. The cows simply separated the good hay from the bad and ate the good stuff. Still the moldy hay remained.

Then the farmer noticed something strange. Even though there was plenty of grass in the paddock, the cows would often be seen pushing their heads between the wires of the fence to eat the grass just outside the paddock. So the farmer left the moldy hay just outside of the fence, close enough for a cow to reach with a stretch. The moldy hay was all eaten in a couple of days.

Forbidden hay, even when moldy, tastes sweet.

I used this simile to help a good friend who had a problem with her husband. He was a good man but never saw the point in religion, not even in meditation. She told me that he would surely benefit from the practical Buddhist teachings if he would take the time to hear them, but he just wasn't interested. So she asked for my help.

"Easy," I said, "just buy one of my books. Take it home and, when you see your husband, tell him to keep his hands off *your* book. Firmly forbid him from reading it."

This she did.

Of course, one day soon after, when she was out shopping and her husband was at home alone, her husband thought something like: "What does she mean by forbidding me from reading her book!"

Then he picked up the forbidden book, read the first story, and did not put it down until he had completed the last tale. Now he comes to my temple every week.

82. The Bully

Wherever there are hierarchies, there will be those who deliberately try to intimidate or persecute those who are weaker. There are bullies in the schoolyard, bullies in the workplace, and even bullies in a monastery, as the following anecdote describes.

In my first year as a monk, while I was squatting on the ground after lunch washing my alms bowl and spitoon, a more senior monk strode up to where I was sitting, loomed over me with monstrous menace, and screamed, "*Brahmavamso*! That is a *filthy* habit! You should *not* wipe your alms bowl with the same cloth that you use to wipe the spitoon! Stop it *at once*!"

Junior monks are expected to show deference to their seniors, but this was too much. The senior monk was trying to intimidate me. Moreover, every other monk was doing what I was being rebuked for. It was unfair, picking on me.

Fortunately, I had the answer for this bully. I calmly did what he asked.

Even though I was churning inside, I used all my powers of self-restraint to keep my mouth closed, walked slowly to where some rags were kept, picked one up, returned even slower to my seat, and wiped the waste vessel with the rag. All the while, I felt the eyes of the many other monks following me. Then I looked up at the bully. All the other monks looked at him as well. They were waiting to see how he would react to my unexpected compliance. All was still for a long two minutes, at the end of which his face went a red brighter than a fire engine. Then he retreated. He never tried that on me again.

Bullies want to prove that they are superior to you. In a spiritual community, such as a monastery, the above method works only when the bullying occurs in public. In an office or a school, or in a private setting, it may be perceived that you are just weak and deserve to be dominated. So if you cannot outsmart the bully or stand up to them, report them to their superiors.

The goal should be to prove that you are at least their equal in wisdom and courage, if not better than them.

83. Bureaucrat Bullies

Government departments are notorious bullies. They have the power, and they often feel the need to demonstrate it.

An Australian Buddhist, who was a member of the Tactical Response Group (SWAT team) of the Western Australian police force, was at an Australian consulate in Asia trying to get a visa for his wife. The official was so unhelpful that he politely complained. She replied, "See that security guard over there! One more complaint out of you, and I will tell him to shoot you!"

Being experienced in hostage situations, he successfully negotiated his way out of trouble, but he told me that he never expected to have to use such skills as an Australian in an Australian consulate.

A second example involves a friend who owns a car repair shop in Perth. When he arrived at his workshop one morning, he could not get into his premises, as a car was illegally parked across his driveway, completely blocking all access. Nor could any staff or customers get in or out. So he called the local council to have the vehicle removed.

The officer at the council explained that they would send a council official to put a sticker on the car but, according to the regulations, they could only tow it away after one week.

"That would mean my customers would be unable to bring their cars in or take them out when they are repaired. My business will have to close for the next seven days!" complained the owner.

"I am sorry, but regulations are regulations," said the government worker.

Fortunately, my friend was smart and courageous. He drove his van to the council offices and carefully parked it across the exit to their parking garage, so no cars belonging to council officers, nor delivery vans and visitors' cars, could come out. When the officials asked him to move his large van, he replied, "Just put a sticker on it. It will be moved, according to your regulations, in seven days' time!"

After brief negotiations, the car blocking his business was swiftly relocated, and shortly after, so was his own van blocking the council's garage.

That's one way to deal with bureaucrat bullies.

84. A Boardroom Bully

Jane, a friend in Sydney, had started her own small business. A big company in the UK became interested in her products and entered negotiations toward a lucrative deal. Soon she received an email requesting her to come to London as soon as possible to sign the contract. This would be the big break for her business that she had dreamed of.

Jane had a cute little baby called Erica. Even though it was hard to leave her very young daughter for a few days, the deal was too important for her family's future to let slip.

Jane booked the first available flight to London and, when she arrived, had only enough time to check in to her hotel, shower, and get changed before getting a taxi to the company's head office. When she walked into the boardroom, the other directors were waiting but not the CEO.

"You have wasted your time," one of the directors told Jane. "You may as well take the next plane back to Australia. Our CEO is in a filthy mood. No way is he going to approve your contract. Go home!"

Jane was not going to give in that easily, especially having traveled halfway around the world for this meeting. "If it is all the same to you," Jane said defiantly, "I will wait to see the CEO myself." Then Jane sat quietly on a chair in the corner of the boardroom.

Jane was a meditator. Her preferred method was meditation on loving-kindness. She was joyfully generating the emotion of compassion to all beings when the CEO burst into the room.

"Who the *hell* is *that*?!" screamed the CEO on seeing Jane sitting so still with her eyes closed. "What does she think she's doing in *my* boardroom?!"

Meditation makes you so calm that even exploding CEOs do not rattle you. Jane calmly stood up, walked toward the volcanic alpha male with neither fear nor arrogance, and told him, "You have such beautiful blue eyes, just like my baby Erica back in Sydney."

Jane told me that those words just came out of her mouth by themselves, with no prior thought at all. The effect was stunning. The CEO did not know what to make of this. His brain had blown a fuse. He stood there for over a minute drowning in complete confusion. The intense expression of anger melted in front of Jane's eyes, and the CEO finally said, smiling, "Really?"

Jane's contract was signed within the next five minutes, and the shell-shocked CEO left the room. Jane then went to leave the boardroom to take a well-earned sleep after such a long journey, but the other directors surrounded her.

"How on earth did you do that? We've never seen anything like that before. Before we let you go back to the hotel, you have to teach us what you did!"

85. I Am Not Good Enough

Most bullies have low self-esteem. They try to compensate for their own lack of self-worth by dominating another. It makes them feel higher when they intimidate someone else.

The Buddha revealed that there are three forms of conceit.

1. Thinking that one is better than someone else
2. Thinking that one is worse than someone else
3. Thinking that one is the same as someone else

The second form of conceit, often unrecognized as a "conceit," is the main cause of bullying. If we could only stop judging each other, then we might stop judging ourselves. As a result, the need to bully, verbally or physically, would be much reduced.

At a reception, a well-dressed guest proudly introduced himself to the host as a doctor.

"I'm a doctor too," said the host warmly. "I'm in general practice."

"Only a GP? I am a brain surgeon," said the guest, raising his nose. "Being a GP is hardly brain surgery!"

"I too am a doctor," said the host's wife. "I work for *Medecins Sans Frontieres* and have just returned from six months treating injured children in a war-torn region of the Middle East. It was extremely dangerous work, but someone has to help those poor kids."

"It must be difficult doing charity work," replied the self-important guest, holding his nose even higher, "but you must admit, it is hardly as difficult as being a brain surgeon!"

"I am a doctor as well," interrupted the host's son. "I have a PhD in physics, and I work for NASA building rockets. You must admit, Doctor, brain surgery is hardly rocket science!"

Then the well-dressed guest's nose fell down, together with his self-satisfaction.

If you find joy thinking that you are better than someone else, then you will find suffering in equal proportions when you meet someone better than you. It is better not to compare yourself at all.

86. I Am Good Enough

When you have a healthy sense of self-worth, then you don't need to play the "I am better than you" game. You don't need to prove yourself. A healthy sense of self-worth comes from realizing the true meaning of being perfect.

A woman walked in a forest looking for a perfect tree. All she saw were crooked trees, trees with missing branches, and trees with damaged bark. Then she went into a government-managed plantation, where she saw all the trees perfectly arranged in rows and lines, perfectly straight, with all the branches perfectly in place.

She realized that the damaged trees in the natural forest were far more beautiful and calming than the "perfect" trees in the artificial plantation. Then she also understood that so-called damaged people are so much more beautiful than artificial people.

She began to feel at home with herself, as much as she felt at home in the natural forest with all the gnarled and crooked trees.

She understood the real meaning of perfection. She had been for a long time "good enough." Only in the forest did she realize it.

87. The Answering Machine

Monks like to spend their time meditating rather than answering the phone. Some people assume that monks have nothing else to do all day than man—I mean "monk"—the phone, answering every caller's problems about marriage and mental health or about giving blessings. I call this the "Dial-a-Monk Service."

So we recorded a new voicemail message at our monastery:

"If you want to hear a recorded blessing chant for good luck, press 1.

"If you want to speak to one of the monks, you are out of luck, so press 1 anyway!"

Now we can meditate in peace.

88. You Have the Right Not to Be Happy

In today's world, if you are not happy, then some assume that there must be something very wrong with you. You need therapy. You may be encouraged to visit a happiness clinic. Some companies even have a "chief happiness officer" to rid their staff of the perceived problem. Happiness is the must-have commodity of the modern age. Soon there will be fines for those who dishearten others by being unhappy in public and jail terms for those serial offenders who are persistently miserable!

Recently, when I was teaching a retreat in beautiful surroundings with very delicious food, a young woman confessed to me that she felt grumpy for no reason.

"I know I should not be unhappy, because I am upsetting everyone else, but I can't help it. I just feel miserable," admitted the girl, guiltily.

So I went to my office and quickly composed and printed out the following "grumpy license":

GRUMPY LICENSE

This document officially grants to the bearer
a perpetual right to be grumpy,
for any reason or no reason at all,

without let or hindrance.
Let no one infringe this right.
Signed, Ajahn Brahm

When I handed her the license to be grumpy, she started laughing.
"You are missing the point!" I protested.

89. The Happiness License

I have also had to print out many happiness licenses. We have to get a license to drive a car, get married, own a dog, and many other things in the modern world—why can't we obtain a license to be happy?

There are many people who think that they do not deserve to be happy. Perhaps they have done some terrible thing in the past for which they cannot forgive themselves. Or maybe they have suffered abuse from another and have lost their sense of self-worth.

At a retreat that I was teaching in Germany, a young man was having trouble meditating. He told me that he was also experiencing many other problems in his life. He couldn't hold down a steady relationship. His career was going nowhere. And he felt that he was living in an endless winter of gloom. Whenever any opportunity for happiness came along, he would habitually chase it away. He subconsciously believed that he did not deserve to be happy. There are many people like him.

I did notice that he had a great respect for me. His friends told me that he regarded me as his all-knowing, all-loving, spiritual master! That was rather excessive, but an advantage nevertheless. I gave him a happiness license, signed by someone he considered infallible. Me!

He respected that license so much that he took it seriously. He framed it and put it on his wall. It was a constant reminder that he had been permitted by someone in authority to be happy. Consequently, he stopped rejecting moments of joy and allowed himself to be happy. Many of his difficulties, including in meditation, vanished.

The only trouble was that he told a friend who posted a copy of my happiness license on Facebook. I was soon inundated with so many requests for signed happiness licenses that I lost my own happiness for a while, having no time to meditate!

So I've put an official happiness license at the back of this book. You can insert your name, cut it out, and put it in your wallet if you want to keep with you a reminder to let yourself be happy. I've given each one my seal of approval!

90. HOW MUCH ARE YOU WORTH?

A few years ago, I was flown all the way from Australia to England to deliver a keynote speech at a prestigious human resources conference in London's Docklands. The fully sponsored trip also meant that I could visit family and friends in the UK.

Fifteen minutes before I was to go up to the podium for the one-hour presentation, one of the organizers told me that there were two people at the entrance to the convention center claiming to be my relatives and trying to get in for free. I went with the manager to check and, sure enough, it was my brother and his daughter. After a minute of sweet-talking, which I am very accomplished at, I convinced the event coordinator to let them in for no charge.

After my session, I scolded my brother and niece for embarrassing me.

"You are a bank manager, brother! And you have a good job too, niece! Why didn't you just pay the fee?"

Then they told me that the fee was three hundred pounds each just to listen to me for sixty minutes.

My annoyance disappeared when I learned how much I was worth. It was replaced by a huge boost in self-esteem.

When I returned home to Australia, I told the committee of my temple about the newly discovered "market rate" for attending one of my talks. They replied diplomatically that I was worth far more than three hundred pounds per hour per person. "You are priceless," the committee proposed, seconded, and unanimously agreed upon. That means they still don't charge anyone to attend any of my talks.

So how much are you worth? Same as me, you are "priceless."

A week after my return, I received another invitation to give a keynote address, this time at the annual convention of the British National Health Service in Birmingham, UK. Again, the organizers would pay all the costs. I declined, arguing that it is very unhealthy to make such long trips too frequently and so, as they were the British National Health Service, it would be hypocritical of me to attend.

91. The power of silence

In the past few years, the price of gold has increased enormously. Because "silence is golden," then silence must be even more valuable today than ever. As a commodity becomes rarer, its value increases.

It is rare to find places of silence in today's world. When I was a youth in London, I would often go into one of the many churches or cathedrals in the city, not to pray that it stopped raining or anything like that, but just to find a sanctuary of silence in which to calm my overactive brain and restore some peace of mind.

The last time that I sought such solace was after a busy day in the city when I entered the vast Westminster Abbey just to meditate quietly for half an hour. As soon as I entered, I was so disappointed. A week or two beforehand, a public address system had been installed with recorded sermons and announcements broadcast continuously. There was no silence any more. I considered this sacrilege and left.

As a result of that experience in Westminster Abbey, I have valued silence so highly that I have tried to create havens of silence in the monasteries and temples that I have influence over, and I have preserved those quiet refuges assiduously.

The building inspector of our local government made an appointment to see me. I thought that there might be some problem with our monastery structures, but he soon dispelled all such concerns. He had just come to thank me.

He told me that he had been working for many years for our local council as the official who gave the final approval on all the new building projects as well as renovations. It was a very stressful job, as builders wanted to cut corners and he had to insist on safety and quality. Whenever he felt stretched past the limit, he would get in his car, drive to our monastery, and park his car in the parking lot. He wouldn't need to get out of his vehicle; just sitting there soaking in the silence was sufficient to relieve all his tiredness and tension.

He had spent many hours unwinding in our monastery parking area. It had been his secret refuge from the stress of his job. He then told me that he was about to retire. Before he left, he had to come and express his gratitude for the silence of our parking lot.

Monasteries where the monks meditate quietly, as opposed to those where they bang drums and ring monstrous bells many times each day, develop a palpable aura of peace. After many years, let alone centuries, that silence becomes as solid as the temple bricks that soak it in day after day, as comforting as a warm mug of soup on a cold night, and as soft and reassuring as a loving hug. Sermons and wise words aren't necessary. Silence is the teacher and the healer.

A friend told me of the time he visited a quiet temple in Bangkok. As he entered the precinct, he noticed a woman sitting alone on a bench, sobbing. Not knowing Thai culture, he felt too uncomfortable to offer any assistance. Instead he went into one of the buildings to complete his own errand.

Half an hour later, when he came out, he saw that woman still sitting on the bench, but now no longer crying. So he went up to her to ask if she needed any help.

The woman spoke good English. She explained that she had just experienced a tragic event and was so distressed that she came to the monastery to calm herself down. She didn't need counseling from any of the monks, nor did she need any help from the stranger. Having found this quiet bench and having had the freedom to cry for as long as she needed, without anyone interrupting her, she now felt so much better. Then she smiled and got up to leave.

"What was the tragedy, if I may ask?" inquired my friend.

"Oh," she replied, "I lost my car keys."

92. inner silence

The famous founder of Taoism, Lao-tzu, would go on a walk every evening accompanied by one of his students. Lao-tzu held a strict rule that the student must not speak during the walk.

On one occasion, a new student was granted the honor of accompanying Lao-tzu on his walk. That day, the master and his disciple reached a ridge in the mountains just as the sun dropped below the horizon. The western sky was streaked with deep crimson, gold, and yellow, like fluttering banners for some celestial celebration.

The young student, in awe at the natural spectacle, burst out excitedly, "Wow! What a beautiful sunset!"

He had broken the strict rule of silence.

The master quietly turned around and walked back to the monastery. Once he had returned, Lao-tzu decreed that the young student could never again accompany him on a walk. He had broken the rule.

The young man's friends tried to intercede for him. After all, it was only one sentence. What was wrong with commenting on such a glorious sunset anyway?

Lao-tzu explained: "When my student spoke, he was not seeing the sunset any more. He was only noticing the words."

There is a fundamental difference between perceiving a description of something and experiencing the thing itself. It is just like the difference between a signpost and the place it is pointing to. Thinking is not the same as knowing.

So how do we achieve inner silence? Most people are so addicted to thought that they claim that they cannot stop thinking. The following exercise shows how easy it is to establish silence within, and how delightful it feels:

1. Sit comfortably, close your eyes, and relax your body for a minute or two.
2. Instead of indulging in thought, voicelessly recite to yourself the phrase "Namo tassa" over and over again for a minute.
3. Next, start to put pauses between the syllables: Na . . . Mo . . . Tas . . . Sa . . . Na . . . Mo . . . Tas . . . Sa . . . and so on.
4. Gradually increase the length of the pauses: Na . . . . . . Mo . . . . . . Tas . . . . . . Sa . . .
5. If thoughts come in between the pauses, shorten the spaces: Na Mo Tas Sa. This will crowd out the thoughts. Then try lengthening the pauses again.
6. Soon the spaces between the syllables will become long, and in those spaces, you will experience for yourself the indescribable inner silence.

It doesn't matter what *namo tassa* means. It is better that you don't know. Otherwise, it will start you off thinking again.

93. when There is no silence

In my first year as a monk in northeast Thailand, the local village held a three-day-long party. Electricity had yet to reach the village, but petrol-driven generators, amplifiers, and huge loudspeakers certainly had. Although the village was over a kilometer away, the sound of the party was disturbing the precious serenity of our monastery.

Buddhism has always taught a "live and let live" philosophy, but when the party was still at full volume at 2:00 in the morning, we resolved to ask for a "sleep and let sleep" compromise. After all, we monks had to rise at 3:00 to start our monastic day.

We asked the headman if they could stop at 1:00, thereby giving us two hours of sleep at night. The answer was a polite no. So we sent a delegation to see our highly revered teacher, Ajahn Chah, and requested that he tell the villagers to turn down the volume at 1:00. We knew that the headman would follow whatever Ajahn Chah said.

It was on this occasion that Ajahn Chah taught us that "It is not the sound that disturbs you. It is you who disturb the sound!"

That wasn't what we expected, but it worked.

The noise would still reverberate in our eardrums but no longer in our minds. We made peace with the inconvenience. It was only three days and soon passed.

Many years later, one of the monk's brothers visited our monastery in Australia. Unfortunately all the guest rooms were full, so the monk asked me if his brother could share his room, just for one night. After all, they had grown up together sharing a room.

"Ah, but you are both much older now," I pointed out. "You probably both snore." The monk insisted there would be no problem, so permission was granted.

The monk's brother fell asleep first and, as predicted, snored so loud that the monk could not get to sleep. Exhausted and sleepless, the monk remembered the advice he had been given. "It is not the sound that disturbs you. It is you who disturb the sound!"

So he started to play with his perception of the snoring, overlaying the sound with imagining it was a soothing melody from a famous classical composer. He could not change the sound of snoring, but he could change the way he perceived it.

When he woke up the next morning, the last thing he remembered, before falling into a refreshing sleep, was how melodious had become his brother's snoring!

So if you have a husband who snores, imagine you are listening to the Grateful Dead or whatever music you like. When the dog barks in the middle of the night, perceive it as an interpretation of Tchaikovsky's *1812 Overture* or something similar. When you can't escape the noise, try changing your perception of it.

94. The In-Between Moments

Much of life is spent having left somewhere but not yet arrived. These are the "in-between moments of your life." They are too often wasted.

Before I was a monk, while I was teaching in a high school, a fellow teacher told me that he had applied for a much better job. He had secured the position but now had to wait a long six months for his teaching contract to expire before starting his dream job. He said that he was surprised and anguished to find himself wishing away a whole six months of his life.

"My life is too short to write off the next half year until I start the new job, but that is what I found myself doing!"

How much of your life has been wasted wishing away hours, days, and months waiting for something to happen: the aircraft to leave, the workday to finish, or the baby to be born? Unfortunately, most of our life is spent in such in-between moments.

Once it is recognized how so much of life is wasted, the tragic "murder rate" in society will decrease significantly. Not so many people will be killing time.

No more will we focus so intently on getting to the destination. Instead we will find new value in the journey, be able to relax in the traffic jam, be willing to speak to fellow commuters on the train, and discover the many adventures that only occur in those precious in-between moments of our lives.

95. Are You a Human Being or a Human Going?

It is very rare to find a human being today. They are always going somewhere, hardly ever being here. That is why I call them "human goings." We have lost the art of just being.

One weekend in my Buddhist temple, I was busy with administration work when an old friend asked me how things were going.

"I'm getting there," I answered.

"Where is it that you are getting to?" he continued wisely.

I immediately got the point and stopped rushing around.

"You have caught me out," I answered, a little ashamed. "I guess the only place I am getting to, rushing around like this, is an early grave!" We both smiled.

If you are one of those "human goings," ask yourself, "Where am I going to? And when will I arrive, if ever?"

As for me, I've already arrived. I've made it to here, and I can now call myself a human being. "Here" is a very comfortable place. I recommend that everyone visit and stay a while, instead of always running away from here, perpetually going somewhere else.

Now, when my friends ask me how things are going, I reply, "I'm just being here!"

96. Don't Worry, Be Hopey

Anxiety is looking at the future and considering all the things that could go wrong. Such unnecessary worry is a cognitive sickness of epidemic proportions in our modern world.

The antidote is looking at the future considering all the things that could go right. It actually increases the likelihood of success. It's adding hope rather than negativity to your future. So don't worry. Be hopey!

A long time ago, a wise but unorthodox spiritual leader taught that there were only two religions to be found in the world:

1. Those that bend the truth to fit their faith
2. Those that bend their faith to fit the truth

He was a follower of the second religion, always ready to abandon a dogma or ritual, no matter how cherished, if well-established facts did not support it.

He was never short of enemies among the traditionalists. Soon his foes found the means to destroy him.

He gave so many public talks, his foes accumulated statements he had made, portrayed them out of context, and accused him of heresy. At the trial, he was found guilty, and the penalty was death!

After the sentence of capital punishment was handed down, the spiritual leader sighed, "Oh, what a pity! I was planning to teach the wife of His Honor the judge a simple form of meditation so that she won't argue with him ever again. Now I will not be able to teach her to be compliant. What a pity!"

"Do you know a method of meditation that can make my wife not argue with me?" asked the judge, intrigued.

"I know all types of meditation, Your Honor," he replied.

"Hmm," considered the judge. "All right. I will grant you a stay of execution for twelve months so that you may teach my wife not to argue with me. But if she is still argumentative after one year, I will personally attend your execution. Court is adjourned."

As the spiritual leader left the courtroom, a free man for twelve months, his disciples asked him what this powerful method of meditation was that could make wives stop arguing with their husbands.

"I don't know," replied the spiritual leader. "I haven't found such a method yet, but I might! Anyway, who knows what may happen in the next year? The judge's wife might die, and that will stop her arguing with the judge—ha ha! Or else I myself might die of natural causes. Whatever, I now have twelve months of freedom. Remember the saying: Don't worry, be hopey!"

97. Being a visitor, Not an owner

Visitors to my monastery would often tell me how tranquil and beautiful the monastery is. I would think they were crazy! Couldn't they see how much work needed to be done? The buildings and grounds had to be maintained. The young monks had to be trained. And the endless questions of those visitors had to be answered. To me, the monastery was a busy work-camp. Something was wrong. I soon realized that it was my attitude.

So I changed my attitude.

One morning each week, usually on a Monday morning, I pretend to be a visitor, not an owner, in the monastery where I have lived for thirty years. As a visitor, I do not have to worry about maintaining the buildings and grounds. Teaching the monks is no longer my business. And, as a visitor, I don't have to answer all those questions. On such mornings, I can appreciate this monastery just as a visitor can. I have found that the visitors are right. It is a beautiful and tranquil monastery, when you don't own it.

I teach this same method to my friends. For a few hours every week, maybe on the weekend, pretend that you are a visitor in the house in which you live.

When you visit others' homes, do you wash the dishes for them? No! Do you vacuum their carpets and tidy up? No! Do you mow their lawn? No! And you don't feel guilty about not doing any of these chores either, because you are a visitor, not an owner.

So when you pretend to be a visitor in your house, not an owner, then you can enjoy its beauty and tranquility. You can rest without feeling guilty. You can enjoy the home with nothing to do. You are just visiting.

Only a visitor can let go. An owner has to control.

98. Don't Just Be Mindful, Be Kindful

A wealthy woman went to her meditation class one evening. Many of her neighbors had been robbed, so she told the guard at the gate to her mansion to be alert and mindful at all times.

When she returned, she discovered that her mansion had been robbed. She scolded her guard, "I told you to be mindful of burglars. You have failed me."

"But I was mindful, ma'am," replied the guard. "I saw the burglars going into your mansion, and I noted 'Burglar going in. Burglar going in.' Then I saw them coming out with all your jewelry, and I mindfully noted 'Jewelry going out. Jewelry going out.' Then I saw them going in again and taking out your safe, and I mindfully noted again 'Safe being stolen. Safe being stolen.' I was mindful, ma'am."

Obviously, mindfulness is not enough! Had the guard been kind to his employer as well as mindful, he would have called the police. When we add kindness to mindfulness we get "kindfulness."

A few years ago I had food poisoning. Monks of my tradition depend on almsfood, offered every day by our lay supporters. We never really know what we are eating, and we often put into our mouths something the stomach later has an argument with. An occasional stomachache is an occupational hazard for monks. But this time, it was far worse than a bout of indigestion. This was the agonizing cramps of food poisoning.

Instead of going to the hospital, which a sensible monk would have done, I used kindfulness.

I resisted the natural tendency to escape from the pain and felt the sensation as fully as I could. This is mindfulness—experiencing the feeling in the moment, as clearly as possible, without reacting. Then I added kindness. I opened the door of my heart to the pain, respecting it with emotional warmth. The mindfulness provided me with feedback. I noticed that my intestines had relaxed a little because of the kindness, and the pain was slightly less. So I continued with the kindfulness. Little by little, the pain decreased as the kindness did its job of relaxing the digestive tract. After only twenty minutes, the pain had gone, totally. I was as healthy and relaxed as if the food poisoning had never occurred.

That was full-on food poisoning. The cramps hurt like hell and made me double up in agony. But it was countered by full-on kindfulness. I have no idea what happened to the bacteria that are the cause of food poisoning, but I didn't worry about that. The pain had gone completely. This is but one personal example of the power of kindfulness.

Kindfulness is the cause of relaxation. It brings ease to the body, to the mind, and to the world. Kindfulness allows healing to happen. So don't just be mindful, be kindful.

99. Kindfulness When You Are Broke

Thomas (not his real name) had spent many months meditating in our monastery in Australia before returning to his home in Germany to pursue further studies. He told me this story of how kindfulness had made him twenty euros when he really needed it.

On Thomas's first day on the campus of a German university, an ATM machine emitted a strange sound as he passed. "A type of gurgling sound," as he described it. He imagined that the university ATM was welcoming him to campus.

From that day on, Thomas repeatedly sent thoughts of kindness to his friend, the ATM, whenever he passed it: "May your bank notes never run out," "May your customers never hit you when they discover they have no funds," "May you never suffer a short circuit," and so on.

After many months, Thomas was sitting in the warm sun having his lunch within a few feet of his friend, the ATM, when he heard the familiar gurgling sound again. He turned around to see a twenty-euro note emerge from the machine!

He had been by the ATM for at least fifteen minutes and no one had come close to the machine, let alone tried to make a withdrawal. He went to the machine, took the note, and then waved it in the air to see if anyone claimed it. No one did. Thomas, the poor student, said "Danke" to his friendly ATM and pocketed the cash.

I repeatedly interrogated Thomas as to the truth of that tale. He vehemently insisted it was true so many times that I now believe him. So please be kind to ATMs, and who knows, one day they may be kind to you!

100. Kindfulness and stillness

Many people try to practice meditation these days. Their biggest problem is that they cannot keep their mind still. No matter how hard they try, they are unable to stop thinking. Why?

A woman received a call one afternoon, "Hi, this is C. F. Are you free this afternoon for a cup of coffee?"

"Sure," the woman replied.

"Good," continued C. F. "We will go that coffee shop that I like, not the one that you prefer. You will have a short black, not one of those high-cholesterol lattes that I know you like. You will have a blueberry muffin, just like me, not one of those silly pastries that I have seen you eat so often. We will sit in a quiet corner because that is where I want to sit, not out on the street where you always go. Then we will discuss politics, which is what I like to talk about, not that spiritual mumbo jumbo that you always twitter on about. Lastly, we will stay for sixty minutes, not fifty minutes nor seventy minutes, just exactly one hour, because that is how long I want to stay."

"Umm . . ." replied the woman thinking quickly, "I just remembered that I have to see my dentist this afternoon. Sorry, C. F., I can't make it."

Would you like to go out for a cup of coffee with someone who tells you where to go, what to eat and drink, where to sit, and what to discuss? No way! And in case you haven't figured it out yet, C. F. stands for Control Freak.

Compare this to someone meditating. "Mind, listen up! We are going to meditate now. You are going to watch the breath, which is what I want to do, not wander off wherever you want. You are going to place your awareness on the tip of the nose, which I like to do, not outside on the street. And you are going to sit there for exactly sixty minutes, not a minute more or less."

When you are the control freak who treats your mind like a slave, no wonder your mind always tries to escape from you. It will think of useless memories, plan something that will never happen, fantasize, or fall asleep—anything to get away from you. That is why you can't keep still!

The same woman receives a call, "Hi! K. F. here. Would you like to come for a coffee this afternoon? Where would you like to go? What would you like to drink and eat? We'll sit where you like, talk about your favorite topics, and stay as long as you like."

"Actually, I have a dentist appointment this afternoon," replies the woman. "Heck! Never mind the dentist. I'm coming to have coffee with you." Then they have such a relaxed and enjoyable time together that they stay much longer than anyone expected. K. F. stands of course for Kindfulness Freak.

What if you meditate by treating your mind like a best friend: "Hey buddy! Do you want to meditate now? What do you want to watch? How do you want to sit? You tell me how long." When you treat your mind with kindfulness, your mind does not want to wander off any-where. It likes your company. You hang out together, chilling out, for far longer than you ever expected.

101. No Fear

One evening, just after dusk, I was meditating alone in one of the last stretches of natural jungle in northeast Thailand. It was getting dark, and the village was many miles away. A monk can become very still meditating far away from people and surrounded only by nature. I could hear only the evening sounds of the forest. I felt comforted by the reassuring background hum, which I knew well by this time, and soon became very peaceful.

That was until I heard the sound of an animal approach.

Most animals in the Thai jungles were benign. But there were also tigers, bears, and elephants in that forest. They were all capable of doing serious injury to people, even killing them. We were told scary stories about these very dangerous killers. The old villagers used to tell me that the big animals usually left the monks alone, but I was not reassured. I figured out that the villagers would never know about those monks who were not left alone by the tigers, elephants, and bears because they would not live to tell the story of their deaths!

To be on the safe side, I carefully listened to the animal that was approaching in the dark. By its sound, it was only a small creature and therefore nothing to worry about. So I resumed my meditation.

The animal came closer and the noise got louder. I became concerned. I mindfully listened, used my reason, and realized I had underestimated the size of the creature. From the way I heard it move through the jungle underbrush, it sounded like a midsize animal, maybe a civet cat. That was also nothing to worry about, so I started meditating again.

Then the noise became very loud. I could tell by the crunching of the leaves on the ground and the cracking of twigs of wood that this was a large animal, a very large one, and it was coming right toward me! I stopped meditating. My heart was pounding. I was so scared that I opened my eyes, turned on my flashlight, and started searching for a tiger or an elephant or bear. I was ready to run to save my life.

After a few seconds, I saw it in the beam of my flashlight. It was a tiny forest mouse.

I learned that fear magnifies things. When you are scared, the sound of a mouse seems like a monk-eating tiger approaching. Fear makes a minor sickness appear like the worst cancer, and a rash becomes the bubonic plague. Fear makes everything much larger than it is.

102. The coffin

A man was returning from the temple late one evening. He decided to take the shortcut past the cemetery. He was a scientist and did not believe in ghosts. At least that is what he told his friends.

I don't know why this is, but the lampposts that illuminate the street are always farther apart next to a cemetery. Or perhaps this is just what it seems like. Cemeteries are always spooky at night, whether you believe in ghosts or not.

Having passed the middle of the cemetery, he felt a little better. Then he thought he heard a strange sound, as though something were following him. He dismissed the perception as mere imagination and carried on walking.

But no! Something *was* following him. So he began to walk a little faster. The thing following him sounded like it was walking faster too. Even though he did not want to, trying to convince himself this was a trick of his mind, he looked behind him. That was a *big* mistake!

His eyes widened in horror. His jaw dropped and began to quiver uncontrollably. The blood drained from his face in shock. Following him, only a few meters behind, was a coffin. A vertical coffin, covered with cobwebs and loose soil. Bump! Bump! Bump!

He turned and ran. The coffin came bump, bump, bump after him. It was catching up.

He ran as fast as he could to the end of the cemetery, hoping the coffin would stop there. But no! The coffin continued after him along the suburban street. Bump! Bump! Bump! It was getting closer and closer. He was pouring sweat, willing his legs to go faster, but they would not.

Luckily, his house was close by. He jumped over the garden gate and ran to his house door. The coffin bumped against the gate, harder and harder. Reaching the front door, he took his house keys from his pocket. With a loud "Bump" the coffin broke through the garden gate. He dropped the keys. The coffin came bumping toward him. Terrified he reached for any key in the bunch and tried to put it in the lock. The coffin was almost upon him. Luckily, a key slid into the lock. He opened the door, jumped inside, and slammed the door shut just as the coffin reached the door. Perspiring and shaking, he let out a sigh of relief.

Bump! The coffin started to strike against the door. BUMP! It crashed with more force against the wood. BUMP! The hinges started to give way. In terror, he ran up the stairs to the only room with a lock, the bathroom. At the top of the stairs he turned around to see the coffin, with supernatural force, break down the front door and enter his home. He darted into the bathroom and locked the door. His heart was pounding.

He could hear the coffin come bumping up the stairs. He heard the coffin come crashing against the bathroom door. If the solid front door could not hold off the coffin, the bathroom door surely would give way. BUMP! And the bathroom door did give way. There were no more places to run. The coffin came toward him. Instinctively, he reached for something to throw at the approaching coffin. It was a bottle of medicine from the shelf. The glass bottle smashed on the coffin, and the pungent liquid spread all over the cobweb-covered wood. The coffin stopped. It was a miracle. The coffin ceased.

The bottle had contained cough syrup. Just as the pharmacist had said, "This will stop any coffin."

103. Kind Ghosts

A friend was a poor builder's laborer in Perth. He was helping renovate an old house built on stumps. While cleaning up after everyone else had gone home, he was passing by the outside of the old building when he heard someone say, "Put your hand under here!"

There was no one around, so he thought that he had imagined the voice.

Then he heard it again, "Put your hand under here!" This was not his mind playing tricks. This was real. This was a ghost!

What would you do? Please don't run away. Many ghosts are kind.

So he carefully put his hand in the space between the ground and the raised floor of the house, and pulled out a large tin box. Opening it, he found many thousands of dollars in cash. He suspected that the previous owner, who had died, had hidden the money under the house to avoid paying taxes. The laborer used that money for the deposit on his first house. It was how he got his start in life.

So if you ever hear a ghostly voice say, "Put your hand under here!" you now know what to do.

Another friend lived alone with her dog. She would go for a walk with him in the woods twice a day. She loved her dog as if it were her only child.

One morning, playing with her dog in the woods, she lost her ring. It was not an expensive piece of jewelry, but it held treasured memories for her. She had a reasonable idea where it must have fallen, but no matter how long she searched, she could not find that ring. Disappointed, she gave it up for lost.

Soon after, she forgot all about the ring when her dear dog died. She missed him terribly. Her walks in the forest without his company made her so sad. So she preferred to remain at home. But one strange thing lessened her grief. For many days after the death, she clearly heard him barking in her house. She was not imagining this. The barking was real, and she easily recognized the sound as her dear dog. It made her a little less lonely.

But she could never see the ghost of her dog. She would hear it in another room, rush there, but there was never a dog to be seen.

One day, she was inside her house by the entrance door when she heard the ghost of her dog bark just outside. She quickly opened the door, expecting to see him for sure this time, but again her beloved dog was not to be seen. Something else was there, however. She looked down, and in the very middle of the welcome mat was her lost finger ring. Her deceased dog had found it for her.

Much of her sadness disappeared after that. Death was not as final a separation as she had once thought. From then on, she heard her dog no more.

Tim had migrated to Perth from London. In the middle of one night, alone in his house, he woke up and turned on the bedroom light. Standing at the end of his bed was his old mother.

His mum lived in Essex. He knew that this must be a ghost. However, he wasn't scared at all, he told me. He was so happy and peaceful seeing his mother silently standing there, smiling at her son with unconditional love.

He knew his mum must have died, but he never felt sad. The love coming from his mother's smile smothered any sadness.

The apparition lasted a long time, several minutes. When the ghost eventually vanished, Tim did what any Englishman would do in such a situation. He got out of bed and made himself a cup of tea!

Drinking his tea, the house phone rang. It was his sister in England.

"Tim, sorry to wake you up in the middle of the night, but I have some bad news."

"Yes, I know," Tim interrupted. "Mother has died."

"How on earth did you know?" his sister exclaimed, incredulous. "We have only just returned from the hospital!"

Then Tim described his mother's ghost. It was one of the most welcome and wonderful experiences to see his mother and bathe in her love one last time.

104. Scottish Mist

When I was a student, I spent many summer vacations in the mountainous wilderness areas of northern Scotland. On one cloudless day, I trekked with the warden of the local youth hostel to the top of a nearby peak. The view at the summit was breathtaking.

Being young and energetic, I suggested continuing on to the next peak, but the older warden had had enough. He told me to go alone. That was some bad advice that almost led to my death.

Halfway up the second mountain, some clouds rolled in. When I got close to the summit, the clouds descended so quickly that I was suddenly enveloped in a thick mist. I could see no more than a meter in front of me.

I had heard stories of English visitors like me being lost in the mist for days but had not believed those tales. I believed that I had a good sense of direction, so I simply turned around and went back the way I had come. With the confidence of youth, I was sure I would soon find my way back. As I carefully walked, looking at the ground two feet in front of me, which was as far as I could see, I suddenly saw the ground fall away in front of me. I almost lost my footing and fell over the precipice. I had come within one foot of a vertical cliff, within one step of a certain death.

I realized I was lost in a dangerous wilderness, in a mist that could last for days. I became worried. My confidence evaporated. I was in serious trouble.

Fortunately, I was studying physics at university. I remembered Einstein's theory of general relativity, which also confirms the well-known fact that water travels downhill. So I found a small mountain brook, followed it to a bigger stream, and then followed that down the mountain until I was below the mist. Then I could see the landmarks to give me directions and return safely to the hostel.

Later, I looked at the map to find that the only cliff on that mountain, over a hundred feet down, was in the direction exactly opposite to where I thought I was going. So much for my innate sense of direction!

I use that anecdote to help guide people in their spiritual journeys. We all start off enveloped in the mist of not knowing. Monks and masters, teachers and guides, all tell us which path to follow, but they all say different things. Their advice is so confusing. We have no innate sense of direction.

So I suggest you find a stream, something you can follow that you know goes in the right direction, that will take you below the mist of not knowing, to see for yourself which way to travel further.

That stream is virtue, peace, and compassion. Whatever religion you follow, and even if you follow no religion, these three qualities will lead you to truth. Follow them. And experience the stream of kindfulness become wider and deeper. Soon it will take you beyond the mist of not knowing to where you can see for yourself and find your way home.

105. Bowing

Buddhists are famous for their bowing. Westerners often ask why we bow. I answer that Buddhist bowing is an effective exercise for the stomach muscles so that you don't get so fat!

Becoming more serious, I explain that when we bow to a statue of the Buddha, for example, we bow to the qualities that the Buddha represents to us. My own three bows to a Buddha image are to virtue, peace, and compassion.

When I lower my head to the floor for the first time, I think of *virtue*. Goodness is so important to me that it is easy to worship it. I find so much happiness living in a community of monks that I can trust completely. When I have the privilege of meeting good people, it brings confidence that this world is a good place. Virtue is well worth a bow. Moreover, when I bow to virtue and remember its importance, I find that my own goodness grows. Whatever you worship and remember grows stronger with every prostration.

Next I bow to *peace*. Peace is also important to me, both in the world outside and in the private world of my meditation. Without peace of mind and peace between peoples, there is no happiness to be found. So I worship peace, and my life becomes more serene.

Lastly I bow to *compassion*. Acts of kindness bring warmth and light to the world. They make suffering bearable, even giving it meaning. A life without kindness is not a life worth living. So when I bow to compassion, I become more compassionate.

That is why Buddhists bow.

A few years ago, I was invited by a Christian friend, the chaplain at a top Perth private school, to give the spiritual address at the morning assembly. When I arrived, my friend the chaplain greeted me along with the school principal.

The principal explained the order of proceedings. "We wait until the whole school is assembled and quiet, and then the three of us will walk in. As we enter," he continued, "the chaplain and I will make a small bow to the statue of Jesus, because we are Christians. But as you are a Buddhist monk, you don't have to bow."

I saw an opportunity to make an important point. I turned to the principal, pretended to scowl, and remonstrated, "I demand my right, as a Buddhist, to bow to your image of Jesus!"

The principal was taken aback, allowing me to explain that I would bow to those qualities in Jesus that I, as a long-practicing Buddhist, respect. Obviously, I don't agree with all the Christian teachings, otherwise I would be a Christian not a Buddhist, but I can see plenty that I respect and can worship, and I wanted to bow to that.

Thus it was that the three of us entered the assembly and worshiped the figure of Jesus. Then some months later, the principal visited my Buddhist monastery and worshiped the figure of Buddha.

106. God in Buddhism

Many people today do not like organized religion. That is why Buddhism has become so popular. Go to any ceremony in a Buddhist temple and you'll discover why we qualify as "disorganized religion."

Some people even ask whether Buddhism is a religion at all. The answer is "Yes, Buddhism is a religion. For tax purposes anyway."

But what about the Buddhist idea of God?

At a chaplaincy seminar at our local university, I was co-presenting with a Benedictine abbot who happened to be an old friend. At question time, a well-known Christian in the audience asked me to explain the Buddhist concept of God.

It would have been easy for me to quote ancient Buddhist texts or sayings handed down from my teachers, but that would have taken the question nowhere. So I decided to answer in a way that would go deeper into wisdom and create greater harmony between two of the world's great spiritual traditions.

"My friend Abbot Placid," I began, "who is sitting next to me, has often told me that one of his core beliefs is that everyone is searching for God. I respect my friend so much that I accept the truth of this belief. So what do I and other Buddhists search for?

"We search for peace, compassion, truth, respect, forgiveness, and unconditional love. If that is what Buddhists search for—atheists too, I would add—and if everyone is searching for God, then that is what God must be. It is peace, compassion, truth, respect, forgiveness, and unconditional love. That is the Buddhist understanding of God."

Those of other faiths were happy with my answer.

107. The Enlightenment Game

When asked by a popular Buddhist magazine to write an article on enlightenment, I sent the following spoof on the TV show *Who Wants to Be a Millionaire?* To my surprise, the article was published.

Who Wants to Be Enlightened?

"Welcome Ladies and Gentlemen. Today on ABC (American Buddhist Channel) we present the final of *Who Wants to Be Enlightened?*

"This show is proudly sponsored by Dhyana Corporation Meditation Cushions, the only company that promises 'If you're not enlightened using our cushions in this life, we'll give you your money back in your next life!'

"Now, with a great pleasure that I am not attached to, I introduce our four finalists: Venerable Anna Gami, Geshe Bo De'Sattva, Roshi Sid Arthur, and renowned lay meditation teacher, psychotherapist, and gay and any other rights activist, Amy Tarbha. Please welcome them with a *Sadhu, Om,* or *Mu!*

"For new viewers to the program, here are the rules again. There will be three elimination rounds, where each of Their Holinesses will be tested on their achievement of enlightenment. One finalist will be eliminated and sent back to the source after each round.

"The first round is a question. How do you describe enlightenment?"

Anna: "Enlightenment means having no self. In fact, as the only

Theravada Buddhist here, following the original teachings of the Buddha, I am the purest and most enlightened. I say that if you have realized that you have no self, then be proud of your attainment and tell everyone."

Bo: "Enlightenment to me means being so compassionate to my disciples that I intentionally get very angry at them so that they don't feel so miserably inferior in my presence."

Sid: "Enlightenment means having no attachment. I am so detached that I am not even attached to detachment, hence my cool new Rolex. Check it out! Awesome, isn't it?"

Amy: "Enlightenment to me is having great sex without the delusion of a self that has to feel guilty about anything."

"Thank you, Your Emptinesses, for your unfathomable wisdom. And the first off the wheel and off the show is . . . Anna! And don't ever come back, Anna Gami.

"The test for the second round is who can sit in meditation for the longest time. So, Your Ineffables, after the gong, meditate!" . . . GONGGG!

After only two minutes, Amy opens her eyes and checks her Twitter account. Sid lasts a whole hour. But Bo sits still for so long that the medics on the show decide that he is dead and cremate him. Bo has gone to suchness. The audience give Bo a big round of "Om! Sweet Om!" Now, only Sid and Amy remain.

"The final round, which will decide the winner of *Who Wants to Be Enlightened?*, has arrived. Isn't this exciting! Sid and Amy, I now want you to demonstrate on live TV a psychic power."

Sid closes his eyes, focuses deep within, and with a rush of ecstasy, he floats up into the air like a feather on the breeze. Higher and higher Sid levitates above the stage until the awestruck audience bursts into thunderous applause. So loud is their cheering that it interrupts Sid's concentration, destroying his psychic power and causing him to come crashing back down on the stage. Breaking his neck, he dies instantly. Many in the audience gain *satori*, Sid returns to the ground of all being, and a new koan is born.

With only one contestant remaining, Ms. Amy Tarbha, famous lay meditation teacher, psychotherapist, and every-right campaigner, is declared the winner of *Who Wants to Be Enlightened?* and presented with a special, limited-edition, solid-gold meditation cushion—hell to sit on, but impressive to look at—with GPS to navigate through and beyond all hindrances. She was the only one left found wanting.

I wrote this piece originally for *Inquiring Mind* (Fall 2010) as a bit of fun to destroy the craving to attain, expose the fraudulence of those who publicly claim to be enlightened, and to vacuum up the centuries-old cultural dust that has covered up enlightenment to the point of total obfuscation.

108. The Menu

An erudite professor of philosophy read in his local newspaper that a new five-star restaurant had opened up in town. He quickly called to make a reservation. The restaurant, however, was already so popular that he had to wait for two months for the next available booking.

Eight weeks later, the professor appeared at the five-star establishment wearing a fine suit and immaculately groomed. The maitre d' asked to see his personal identification to confirm that he did indeed have a reservation that night. Seeing that he did, the maitre d' led him to his table.

The professor was in awe at the interior decoration and fittings of the exclusive restaurant. The soft light from the unobtrusive standing lamp bathed his table in a warm, understated glow, reminding him of the calming light of twilight, secretive but just enough to see. A waiter in a white bow tie and elegant jacket presented him with the menu.

Even the menu matched the plush, rich surroundings of the five-star restaurant. It was made of thick, golden parchment with a border of deep crimson. The 108 items on the menu were written in exquisite calligraphy, the sort that is seen in museums of art more than restaurants.

The professor gazed in admiration at the menu, reading it many times. Then he proceeded to eat the menu. After which, he paid his bill, thanked the maitre d', and left.

The unfortunate professor, learned as he was, did not know the difference between the menu and the food. The words were all he knew and cared for.

You, my reader, have now completed the 108 items on the menu that is *Don't Worry Be Grumpy*. Please don't be like the philosophy professor who "eats" only the words.

Happiness License

This document

officially grants the bearer a perpetual right to be happy,

For any reason or no reason at all, without let or hindrance.

Let no-one infringe this right.

Ajahn Brahm

AJAHN BRAHM

About Ajahn Brahm

Ajahn Brahmavamso Mahathera (lovingly known to many as Ajahn Brahm) was born Peter Betts in London, United Kingdom, on August 7, 1951. He came from a working-class background and won a scholarship to study theoretical physics at Cambridge University in the late 1960s. After graduating he taught high school for one year before traveling to Thailand to become a monk and train with the Venerable Ajahn Chah Bodhinyana Mahathera. While still in his years as a junior monk, he was asked to undertake the compilation of an English-language guide to the Buddhist monastic code—the Vinaya—that later became the basis for monastic discipline in many Theravada monasteries in Western countries.

The then Venerable Brahm was invited to Perth, Australia, by the Buddhist Society of Western Australia to assist Ajahn Jagaro in teaching duties. Initially they both lived in an old house in the suburb of North Perth, but in late 1983 purchased ninety-seven acres of rural and forested land in the hills of Serpentine south of Perth. The land was to become Bodhinyana Monastery (named after their teacher, Ajahn Chah Bodhinyana). Bodhinyana was to become the first dedicated Buddhist monastery in the Southern Hemisphere and is today the largest community of Theravada Buddhist monks in Australia.

Initially there were no buildings on the land, and as there were only a few Buddhists in Perth at this time and little funding, the monks themselves began building to save money. So it was that Ajahn Brahm learned plumbing and bricklaying and built many of the current buildings there himself.

In 1994, Ajahn Jagaro took a sabbatical leave from Western Australia and disrobed a year later, abruptly leaving Ajahn Brahm in charge. Despite initial reservations, Ajahn Brahm took on the role with gusto and was soon being invited to provide his humorous and uplifting teachings in other parts of Australia and Southeast Asia. He has been a speaker at the International Buddhist Summit in Phnom Penh in 2002 and at four Global Conferences on Buddhism. He was the convener of the Fourth Global Conference on Buddhism, held in Perth, in June 2006. But such recognition has not stopped him from dedicating time and attention to the sick and dying, those in prison or ill with cancer, people wanting to learn to meditate, and of course his own Sangha of monks at Bodhinyana.

Currently Ajahn Brahm is the abbot of Bodhinyana Monastery in Serpentine, Western Australia, the spiritual director of the Buddhist Society of Western Australia, spiritual adviser to the Buddhist Society of Victoria, spiritual adviser to the Buddhist Society of South Australia, spiritual patron of the Buddhist Fellowship in Singapore, and is currently working with monks and nuns of all Buddhist traditions to establish the Australian Sangha Association.

In October 2004, Ajahn Brahm was awarded the John Curtin Medal for his vision, leadership, and service to the Australian community by Curtin University.

Ajahn Brahm has also written several books, including *Who Ordered This Truckload of Dung?*, *Mindfulness, Bliss, and Beyond: A Meditator's Handbook*, and *The Art of Disappearing*. Over a thousand of Ajahn Brahm's Dhamma talks are now available for free download in both digital audio and video format.

Other Books by Ajahn Brahm from Wisdom Publications

The Art of Disappearing
Buddha's Path to Lasting Joy
160 pages, $15.95. 9780861716685. Ebook 9780861718610.
"This is Ajahn Brahm's prescription for true peace and profound happiness. What a gift of the Dhamma!"
—Toni Bernhard, author of *How to Be Sick*

Mindfulness, Bliss, and Beyond
A Meditator's Handbook
Foreword by Jack Kornfield
304 pages, $16.95. 9780861712755. Ebook 9780861719839.
"Riveting and real. I can't tell you how thrilled I was to read it."
—Glenn Wallis, translator of *The Dhammapada: Verses on the Way*

Who Ordered This Truckload of Dung?
Inspiring Stories for Welcoming Life's Difficulties
288 pages, $15.95. 978086171278. Ebook 9780861719273.
"Ajahn Brahm is the Seinfeld of Buddhism."—Sumi Loundon

About Wisdom Publications

Wisdom Publications is the leading publisher of contemporary and classic Buddhist books and practical works on mindfulness. Publishing books from all major Buddhist traditions, Wisdom is a nonprofit charitable organization dedicated to cultivating Buddhist voices the world over, advancing critical scholarship, and preserving and sharing Buddhist literary culture.

To learn more about us or to explore our other books, please visit our website at www.wisdompubs.org. You can subscribe to our eNewsletter, request a print catalog, and find out how you can help support Wisdom's mission either online or by writing to:

Wisdom Publications
199 Elm Street
Somerville, Massachusetts 02144 USA

You can also contact us at 617-776-7416, or info@wisdompubs.org.

Wisdom is a 501(c)(3) organization, and donations in support of our mission are tax deductible.

Wisdom Publications is affiliated with the Foundation for the Preservation of the Mahayana Tradition (FPMT).